ANNA ÖRNBERG

Country Style

Home Décor and Rustic Crafts from Chandeliers to Coffee Tables, Bedcovers to Bulletin Boards

Bohemian

Industrial

Elegant

Shabby chic

Translated by Ellen Hedström

Skyhorse Publishing

Copyright © 2011 by Anna Örnberg
English Translation © 2014 by Skyhorse Publishing
Photography by Tommy Durath
Design by Monica Sundberg
First published in 2011 as *Inred lantligt på
ditt eget sätt* by Anna Örnberg, Bokförlaget
Semic, Sundbyberg, Sweden

Skyhorse Publishing books may be purchased in
bulk at special discounts for sales promotion,
corporate gifts, fund-raising, or educational purposes.
Special editions can also be created to specifications.
For details, contact the Special Sales Department,
Skyhorse Publishing, 307 West 36th Street, 11th Floor,
New York, NY 10018 or info@skyhorsepublishing.com.

Skyhorse® and Skyhorse Publishing®
are registered trademarks of Skyhorse Publishing,
Inc.®, a Delaware corporation.

www.skyhorsepublishing.com

10 9 8 7 6 5 4 3 2 1

Library of Congress Cataloging-in-Publication
Data is available on file.

ISBN: 978-1-62873-643-4

Printed in China

A big thank you

to everyone who welcomed photographer
Tommy and me into their homes.
Sometimes we took photos of other
people's inspiring homes and other
times we used the space to show off
the things I created.

**Josefine & Andreas
| Malin & Johan | Lena & Per**

**Malin & Niclas | Stina & Per
| Marie & Örjan**

**Marie & Marcus | Kicki & Fredrik
| Pernilla & Peter**

**Paula & Tommy | Mia & Ulf
| Camilla & Jan**

"Systrarna i Fållorna"

And a huge thank you to the

Swedish stores

Panduro

Lunden's Greenhouse

Slöjd-Detaljer

Margareta's Interiors & Presents

for props and material, as well as
advice and help. What would we have
done without you?

Contents

Country Style

—what is it?

Defining country style is not easy, as it encompasses so much, and everyone can interpret the style in their own way.

One thing that characterizes country style is its love of the tarnished look or patina—oh how we adore anything that looks worn, rubbed, corroded, oxidized, rusty, or stamped by the hallmark of time!

An old cupboard with worn and chipped paint makes our heart leap. For the cupboard to satisfy an antiques expert, it has to be an original from the eighteenth century. A "countryphile," however, is just as happy with a newer cupboard that has been tarnished to look old. Some of us even like the cupboard better if it's a half-decent piece from the '40s that we picked up at the thrift store and then painted and patinated.

We also love things that are pleasingly aged, and we love to find such things at thrift shops and antique stores. We go all gooey over simple, old items and strange curios, dented with worn edges and flaking paint.

You could even go so far as to say that those of us who are obsessed with country style don't judge the value of our interiors by how much they cost, and instead measure them by the ambience that these items create. We randomly mix expensive and cheap, old and new, fresh and funky with worn and torn, and we like it that way!

What does it look like?

Mixing it up is key; you don't want to live in a junk store, so your aim is to not make your home a mixed collection of worn and scuffed items. Instead, you should contrast items in order to enhance the charm of the old and worn, rather than let it be overpowering. So let nice clean surfaces, fresh paint, and the shiny and glossy meet the dented, rusty, scratched, and worn.

To mix country with other styles is no more strange than introducing a new word into a language. Country style comes in many guises: it can be tough with an industrial edge, romantic and elegantly stylish, or have a playfully colorful bohemian twist—just like one language might have many dialects.

I have visited many country-inspired homes with my photographer Tommy; for many of them white is the dominant decorating color. It makes for a light and airy environment that is easy to adapt, much like a painter's canvas! Play with contrasting colors, change curtains, hang a new lamp, and suddenly your room takes on a whole new look. Fresh paint on the walls can make magical changes, and a white home, with white furniture in white rooms, gets a dramatic makeover with a wide variety of accent colors. White furniture works with just about everything.

I personally like country style for the fact that it has a strong DIY component. I love the challenge of changing slightly dull furniture using color and detailing. My favorite thing is to find new ways to use old items and to recycle and change the mundane into the extraordinary. My husband often sighs and wonders if I even realize that there are stores selling new things out there. Sure I do, I just don't think they're as much fun and not at all as satisfying as when I do my own hammering, painting, or sewing. I also feel better when I recycle instead of just throwing things away and buying new. I'm happy when I see the results! It's a passion that I am happy to share and I hope that you find this book both inspiring and informative. Make good use of it when you decorate and fix your own home.

Enjoy!—Anna

Casual Country Romance

The philosophy of decorating in the country style is all about enjoying your daily life and taking pleasure in the simple things—adding an edge to everyday activity and seeing the beauty in what's normal.

So what makes the heart race for those who love country style? Designer furniture, expensive art, or the latest media technology? Hardly! More like old kitchen towels, wire art, or rose-patterned tea cups are the things that might be high on the wish list. Everyday objects and ordinary items become beloved decorative items in homes with a country style. We might use modern washing machines, but an old washboard can be still hung on the wall. Visit your nearest thrift store and get some beautiful bargains for a small sum or simply look around you . . . what do you have in your vicinity that deserves pride of place in your home?

MIXED

In country style, expensive art is conspicuously absent, but old school posters are lovingly displayed. Posters featuring old-fashioned drawings of scientific categorizations of flora and fauna are a trend that can be appreciated both by those who prefer a more romantic style as well as by those who like a tougher, more industrial one. A romantic cast-iron bed frame is accompanied by a bedside table made from a tarnished milk churn. Together with a modern lamp, it creates a mix that doesn't come across as too cutesy.

HOW TO HANG TEA TOWELS

Why hide old towels in the closet? Make a clothes line from a piece of string and hang them where you can see them, or pile them high in loosely woven baskets that hang from the ceiling.

STILL LIFE

A jug, old cutlery, and a stack of plates on a small silver tray all make for a charming still life on the window sill or a centerpiece for the kitchen table instead of a bunch of flowers.

CLUTTERED, BUT CALM

On simple, open shelves along the kitchen wall, Paula has placed her collection of white china, wire art, and antique cake molds. Though the items jostle for space, the simple colors are calming. The practical, but less attractive, kitchen items have been hidden behind closed doors so they can be close at hand for daily use.

Pretty as a picture

A mullioned window frame, with or without glass, can be hung up or leaned against the wall to make a decorative piece at a low cost.

Expressive storage

Woven baskets, wooden boxes, and old trunks give a warm, lived-in feel as well as solve your storage problems. Fill them with newspapers, books, candles, and old, rolled-up sheets.

WHITE ENHANCES

A clean, white room enhances details in the same way that the white walls of an art gallery enhance art. Common household and garden items are transformed into effective displays, such as the old milk churn, the pile of wood, or the cupboard door made from an old, weather-worn window frame. The chair is an old pull-out bed that is more of a fun detail rather than a comfortable place to sit.

CANDLES ARE A LUXURY

Lighting a few candles is one of the easiest tricks to create a cozy ambiance. It's a luxury we can all indulge in, so be generous with the wax but careful with the flames. An old chalk-board instead of a table cloth is a unique twist.

BEAUTIFUL THINGS

On the kitchen island we find a quaint collection of small items in a tranquil palette. These items are not only there to look good but are also used on a daily basis. Charming and convenient!

Be a Bookworm

*Shelf upon shelf, brimming boxes,
pile after pile—thrift stores are
bursting with old books in need of a
home. Luckily for you, an old book for
a buck makes cheap material to work
with, and a pile of books can quickly
become various interior decorations.
So be a bookworm!*

PAPER POETRY

It's exciting to browse the shelves for old books. Perhaps you won't find any books you'd like to read, but that doesn't mean you can't find some lovely crafting material instead! Look at the typeface, the type of paper, or language the book is written in. Old covers with a lovely patina or paper marked by age are a bonus, as are old-fashioned black and white illustrations. An ancient arithmetic textbook written in German or an Italian travel memoir about Constantinople may not be what I want to read, but they make beautiful decorations.

With pages from books you can make a poetic wall collage. It's more visually enticing if the pages have various color shades, languages, and typefaces; some text might be close together, others spaced out. Don't cut the pages from the book; rather, tear them carefully to give them a slightly jagged edge. Mount some pages with nails and use masking tape to mount others.

Old books also make lovely decorations just as they are. Stack books on top of each other to make a great presentation. Sometimes you can even find books with lovely images on the cover that you can make into small pictures—mount the entire book on the wall!

LITERATURE ART

A book can be folded and shaped in different ways, and this is a style that takes only minutes to make. Open the book in the middle, take 6–8 pages at a time, and bend them softly into the middle of the book. Repeat as many times as required in order to get the pages to create a fan shape like in the picture above. You don't need to glue it, and you won't harm the book. Just flick the pages back and close the book anytime you want.

BUNCH & BIND

With a little bit of effort, some less interesting books are converted into quaint decorations that evoke feelings of nostalgia. Pull the covers off and peel away the first few pages to get to the title page. This works best with books where the page signatures have been sewn into the spine; newer books are glued, which doesn't make for the same effect. Bunch a few books together and tie them with a piece of rough string or twine that you wind around the bunch a few times.

FOR THE LITERARY GASTRONOME

Make placemats that will give your dinner guests something to talk about! Choose a slightly thicker piece of paper or board, around 12 x 16 inches (30 x 40 cm), and make a collage from the pages of books. Glue them onto the paper. Regular paper glue works just fine. Choose your books with care; pages from old encyclopedias, cookbooks, poetry, or joke and quote books may inspire lively discussions.

Framed pages

Regular printed pages can
be so attractive that they
become works of art in
themselves—especially old
books with pages that have
to be separated by the
reader. They have a lovely
texture with their thick
paper. If you want to make
the pages even stronger,
you can glue them onto
another piece of paper.
Make holes at the top of
the pages using a hole
punch and add a metal
grommet to the holes. The
paper will take on an aged
appearance if you brush an
ink pad along the edge. The
paper can be decorated with
stamps or can be used as a
background for black and
white photos. Thread some
string through the hole and
hang them up—several pages
together are even more
effective. An old window
pane to frame it all
finishes off your creation.

A READING LAMP

. . . or is it a lamp you can read? Of course not! However, with slightly thicker pages you can make your own literary lampshade using layered strips of paper. As a fun addition, every strip has been decorated with an odd button glued on.

MATERIALS

- 1 lampshade ring 10 inches (25 cm) in diameter, 1 mobile ring 8 inches (20 cm) in diameter, and 1 mobile ring 6 inches (15 cm) in diameter (can be found in craft stores)
- 8 pieces of strong wire, 6 inches long (15 cm)
- A book with thick pages
- A brown ink pad
- Glue stick
- A lamp holder with a protective cover so that there is no risk of the bulb coming into contact with the paper. Example: the "Ekarp" lamp holder from IKEA in the picture has the necessary lamp cover.

HOW TO

1. Place the lamp ring, with the help of the lamp holder, at a suitable height. Fold each end of the wire pieces at around 1½ inches (3 cm) to make them into hooks that attach to the lamp rings. Attach one end of four of the hooks onto the lamp ring and distribute the rest evenly. At the other end of the hooks, attach the larger mobile ring and repeat to attach the smaller mobile ring at the bottom.

2. Fold and tear strips from the books, about ½ x 8 inches (4 x 20 cm). The length of the strips should be straight, but the ends that will be visible can be jagged and uneven. Give all the strips a dark border by brushing the edge with an ink pad.

3. Spread some glue along the paper strips' top edges and fold the paper ¾ to 1 inch (2 to 2½ cm) over the lamp/mobile ring. Start with the smallest ring and attach the strips the whole way around, then move onto the middle ring and finally the largest one.

4. On the largest ring, you can attach a further round of slightly shorter paper strips.

THE RUSTLE OF PAPER

Cut thin strips from the pages of a book and scrunch them together to make them wrinkly. You'll get a fluffy pile of paper that can be used as both packing material and as decoration. This little bird made a soft nest of tousled paper underneath a glass cake cover.

BOOK LABELS

Pages from books make more than just lovely packing materials, they also can make fun labels! Tape or glue strips of pages around a collection of glass bottles, then use a darker brown paper so that the names of what's inside are visible. Use these bottles to store your odds and ends.

PICTURE PERFECT COLLAGES

Collages made from the pages of books make a great background for old black and white photos. The collage is attractive in itself while at the same time it enhances the size of whatever picture you may have. In a large collage frame, you can group several old photos together with old letters, postcards, or other memories that are suitable to put on display.

DINING WITH A BOOK

You can make decorative place cards from a small book. Use glitter glue and write the guest's name in large letters over the printed text. If you are lucky, you can find a book with some form of quick entertainment, such as poetry, songs, riddles, and other pieces that lend themselves to being read out loud, if your dinner guests are in the mood.

A LIBRARY TABLE

The most affordable paper there is comes from old books. In addition to its low cost, it's also so decorative that you can use it to decoupage both furniture and other items. This simple little table was given a facelift with some white paint and a checkered pattern made from diamond-shaped paper cut-outs from different books.

HOW TO

1. All surfaces have to be cleaned, sanded, and then wiped free of dust. If the surfaces are treated with a woodstain, you'll need to use a primer specifically for stainblocking, like KILZ 2. The waterbased primer is fast drying. Paint at least three, maybe four or even five coats. Smooth the surface with fine sandpaper. Spend a little extra time sanding the edges and corners until the table gets a slightly worn appearance.

2. Measure the surfaces you want to decorate and calculate the right size for the diamonds or squares you are going to decorate with. Make a template from cardboard and cut the shapes out of different book pages.

3. Use an ink pad of a brown shade to tarnish the paper. Brush the pad along the edges of the paper using a light touch to darken them slightly.

4. With a pencil, draw a line to mark the area that will be decorated so the squares line up straight. Paint some decoupage glue onto the back of the paper. Let it absorb for a few moments, then place it where you want it and lightly press against the surface.

5. Take a smidgen of white paint on a brush and brush lightly over the paper diamonds so the paper gets a light, streaky effect—back and forth. This gives it a beautiful "hazy" look. Finish off by sealing the whole table in a water-based varnish. Choose a crystal clear varnish, one that won't give you any yellow tone, to ensure that the white stays white. Ask at your local paint store for recommended brands.

Books wrapped in brown paper

Even brand-new books can be left out as decoration if their modern covers are hidden by something more subtle, like this crinkled brown paper. First I scrunched the paper tightly into a ball and then smoothed it out again. A bit of white paint on a brush lightly run over the paper enhances the wrinkles. The title of the book has been stamped along the spine, but if your handwriting is neat, don't hesitate to write it by hand!

Silver Shine

Spend a few dollars on silver trays and plates from the thrift store. The old silver will blend well with a country shabby chic style, and it makes a nice contrast against worn and rubbed surfaces.

WALL-MOUNTED CANDLE SCONCES

The idea of this is that the silver should reflect the flame and maximize the light. A serving tray made of silver is perfect for this. Drill a hole in the edge and attach a candle holder like in the image to the left (can be found in select craft stores, online at Panduro Hobby, or you can use a recycled sconce) by screwing it on. Make another hole at the top edge to hang it up or mount it with the help of a plate stand.

MEDALLIONS

Glass coasters are large enough to make into medallions where the silver frames an old picture or a pretty photo. Use them as decorations, attach to a garland, or hang them from branches around the home.

SHINY SILVER WALL COLLAGE

Silver plates and trays make pretty works of art. They reflect the light in the same way a mirror can light up a room. Collect plates and trays in various sizes and shapes and group them on the wall using plate hangers to make an effective wall decoration for hardly any money at all.

CHANDELIER

A large plate can form the base for a shiny chandelier with candles. Hang the chandelier with metal chains that can tolerate the heat from the candles.

HOW TO

1. Under the plate, glue on a smaller, more bowl-shaped plate. It's even better if the smaller plate has a perforated decoration so it's easier to attach the pearls, prisms, and garlands. If it doesn't have holes, you will need to drill holes for these attachments. Use superglue and reinforce the glue by drilling a few small holes between both plates and "sew" them together with some fine-gauge wire.

2. Thread beads onto some fine-gauge metal wire and hang some garlands as décor. The prisms need a slightly heavier gauge wire that can be bent to make a hook to attach them.

3. Glass prisms with a smooth surface can be decorated. You can stamp some decorative lettering or patterns on some white silk paper. Glue the paper using decoupage glue onto the flat side of the prism, and when the glue has dried, excess paper can be removed using a sharp scalpel.

SERVE ON A SILVER TRAY

You can purchase a whole collection of small, silverplated trays or serving plates without spending too much. It's great for parties but also for day to day use, where you can jazz up a regular sandwich with some silver shine.

CLASSY PEDESTAL CANDLE

You can find balusters that have been lathed in many nice profiles and varying dimensions at your local home improvement store, which can be painted in any color and made into the base for a large candle stick. About 8 inches (20 cm) at each end of the pole tends to be straight and square; this is where you saw off the edges at 90 degrees, just keeping ¾ to 1¼ inches (2–3 cm) of the straight part. Turn a large plate upside down and you'll have a nice base that is then attached to the lower end of the baluster, using screws and washers for extra support. Attach a smaller plate at the top of the baluster—also with screws but with no need for washers.

Bonus tip: Use some clear silicon to glue a wide glass bowl or deep dish plate to the small silver plate. Now you have a fancy bowl on a pedestal that you can use to arrange flowers in, or place fruit for that extra-lavish tablesetting.

Wings from a Guardian Angel

Who wouldn't like to have their own set of heavenly wings? In the hopes of getting a real pair some day, you can make your own angel wings for poetic home décor. Wire thread, glue, and paper or a thin fabric are all you need to fill your house with the whispering flutter of angel wings.

Wings

MATERIAL
- Galvanized wire, 14 gauge, 1.5 mm in diameter
- Paper or thin fabric
- Decoupage glue
- Plastic cover to protect your work surface
- Brush and wire cutters

Thin fabric wings

Fabric also works and can be glued together in two layers with the wing's wire frame between the layers. Choose a thin fabric so the wings aren't too heavy for the frame. For example, the wings in the picture were made from cotton voile. The fringed "feathery" edge consists of strips torn from a cotton sheet, approximately 1¼ inches (3 cm) wide, and glued along the bottom wire, overlapping each other slightly. Hide the short ends with a ribbon.

1 square =
³⁄₄" × ³⁄₄" (2 × 2 cm)

1 inch = 2¹⁄₂ cm

OPULENT & OPAQUE

Our fairy wings have a thin, oblong shape inspired by a vintage French wing design. The wire is placed between two sheets of white silk paper, which makes light, translucent wings, but they are also delicate and fragile.

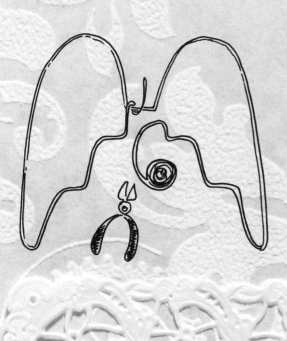

HOW TO

1. Draw the wings you want to make at full size. In between the wings you will need a small "bridge" of around 1–1½ inches (3–4 cm) made from wire. Bend the wire on both sides of the bridge and shape into wings, just like the one you have drawn.

2. When you have bent the wire the whole way around the wing shapes, finish off by winding the remaining wire around the straight bridge.

3. Place a layer of paper or fabric on a covered work surface and apply glue to the whole surface. Place the wire wing on the paper or fabric and then add another layer of paper or fabric. Brush some more glue over the surface to saturate the paper/fabric, which means that any air bubbles will get pressed out.

4. Allow to dry flat, but lift the wings while they are still a bit damp so they don't stick to the surface. Hang them up to air dry.

5. When the glue has set, the paper or fabric will be stiff, which makes it easy to cut clean with an X-Acto knife or razor blade. Cut out the wings from the paper 5–10 mm outside the wire frame. The wire bridge between the wings should be wrapped with a piece of fabric.

A stronger pair of wings

Slightly sturdier wings can be made if you choose normal paper, but then you have to adapt the size of the wings to the size of the paper. We gave our wings a step shape at the bottom.

Lovely Lampshades

Breathe new life into an old lampshade! It's quite simple to give a boring lampshade a new look; with a bit of creativity, you might even make it into something that looks completely different.

PARTY SHADE

Skip the light fixture and just use a large, puffy wire frame to bind it, just because it's decorative and fun. It can be hung up in your home or just used to brighten up a party. Why not hang it over the snack table or maybe use it to spotlight the guest of honor.

HOW TO

Wrap the shade's upper and bottom edges with a garland of fake greenery, flowers, and beads. You can even add some further decorations such as cloth butterflies and artificial flowers. Add a decorative item to the top of the shade; I used a tin flower pot in the shape of a crown. Inside the shade, I hung long strands of beads on a wire with a prism at the end.

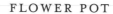

FLOWER POT

Turn a small lamp shade upside down and place a plant in it. It may be a bit kooky but the more out there, shiny, and decorated the lamp shade is, the better. The plant can be placed in a plastic bag and wound with a page from an old book. A small silver-plated dish under the lamp shade is the finishing touch.

PRETTY BEADS

A small wire frame becomes a sparkling jewel when it's decorated with beads. Really go to town with the bling! The beads don't have to be expensive; you can mix seedbeads with faceted beads of colored, transparent plastic. First thread a whole bunch of seedbeads, approx. ⅛ inch in diameter, onto a thin metal wire, then wrap the wire around the frame. For each time you wrap the wire around, one of the small beads is placed along the frame; at the end, you have rows of seedbeads along all the main wires of the frame. The flowers are formed from large loops of tightly strung seedbeads on metal wire.

Silk, velvet, rags

If the wire frame has a pleasing shape, it can be quite sassy to have the frame itself serve as a lamp shade. Wrap strips of fabric around the frame to hide any chipped paint and add some flair to it.

To make a bohemian look, we chose a fabric with colorful flowers on a black base. The fabric was a synthetic mix, which meant that the edges frayed when the material was ripped. This is perfect; it allows for the slightly rough look that we love.

We used 5 fabric strips, 2 x 60 inches (150 cm), to dress the frame. Wrap the material in several layers on top of each other so that the frame gets a fuller, padded look. Attach the ends of the strips with hot glue from a glue gun, or sew them on by hand.

PRIMA BALLERINA

As cute as a cupcake, in delicate tulle netting, this white lamp floats over the table. The best part is that you make this dreamy creation from ripped strips of sheets and tulle without sewing a single stitch!

HOW TO

You need a wire frame, tulle netting, and a white or neutral-colored sheet. Rip 2 inch (5 cm) wide strips from the sheets and 4 inch (10 cm) wide strips from the tulle. The strips should be long enough that they can be placed double around the frame and tied with a double knot along the underside of the frame. Start by tying at least two layers of sheet strips around the frame so that they cover the frame and hide the light bulb. The tulle can then be tied in 2 or 3 layers until you have so many knots that the fabric and tulle form a fluffy, sprawling frill around the frame.

TIP!

In thrift stores you can find lots of fun things to hide less fancy, plastic light sockets. An upside down sterling silver bowl and a little tea light holder shaped like a crown hides the light socket on this ballerina frame as well as serving as that little extra bit of decorative oomph.

Rugged Romantic
With jagged edges & torn strips

1 Romantic collage

2 Rugged rose

3 Folded frills

4 Ripped stripes

5 Patchwork with visible seams

6 Back and forth

7 Scrunched strips

DREAM ON BABE

Rip, tear . . . to rip the edges on fabric feels just great! It looks spontaneous and makes a nice contrast to the romantic lace and frills—a little less cute and a little more edgy.

ROMANTIC COLLAGE

Collect doilies, mother of pearl buttons, an old-fashioned photo transferred onto fabric (yes, it's easy. Fabric transfers can be bought in craft stores or whereever they sell special paper for computer printers. Just follow the instructions on packaging). You can't fail if you use fabric in the same soft, neutral color palette. Sew roughly with scraggly stitches that are slightly too long and sew outside the edges as this makes your collage slightly less refined.

A label made from fabric gives a three dimensional depth to the collage. Tear a thick strip of material and fold it. Sew a tight zigzag seam along the edge, make a hole with a grommet, and thread. a ribbon through. The label can be tied around a button on the cushion. You can choose to decorate the label with a motif or stamped text. Waterproof ink pads work fine on fabric. You can also add buttons, lace, or a label cut from a piece of clothing by sewing them on.

RUSTIC ROSE

A rose by any other name is still a rose, even when it's made of ripped pieces of material and given frayed leaves.

Leaves: Rip 3 inch (8 cm) wide strips of linen cloth and cut into strips 6 inches (15 cm) long. Make a point on the leaf: Fold the strip in half lengthwise and sew a seam along the fold in a soft, gentle curve. Cut away any excess fabric and press the seam.

Place together 2 parts to make a leaf—wrong sides against each other. Sew the "veins" of the leaf with a tight zigzag seam—both to give it a more realistic effect as well as to make it more stable.

Draw a circle, 4 inches (10 cm) in diameter, on the front of a circular cushion. Make a few wrinkles on the lower edge of the leaf and sew it on about a ½ inch (1 cm) outside the drawn circle.

Rose: Tear long strips of linen material 1½ inches (4 cm) wide and scrunch together to make a frill. Sew onto the circle marked on the cushion with a wide zigzag seam along the contour.

The scrunched, curly middle bit is made by hand by turning and twisting the stripped pieces of fabric into a creased fold, while at the same time sewing them on by hand with extra strong thread.

FOLDED FRILLS

Circular frills are made with small wrinkles that you fold as you sew. It's quicker than other methods and looks great. On the front of a circular cushion, 16 inches (40 cm) in diameter, trace up to 4 circles using a pencil—1½ inches (4 cm), 4¾ inches (12 cm), 8 inches (20 cm), and 11 inches (28 cm) in diameter. Tear long strips from a sheet, about 3 inches (8 cm) in width.

Start at the outer circle and sew the strip on with a three-step zigzag seam along the pencil markings while at the same time making ½ inch (1 cm) deep creases along the strip, just in front of the presser foot as you sew—just don't sew too fast.

When you reach the end of the strip, just take a new one and continue sewing onto the creased frill until you have finished the round. Do the same with the next three circles that you have traced until you have four rounds of frills that overlap slightly. Hide the middle of the cushion with a rosette made from 4–6 strips of fabric, folded into figure eights and layered on top of each other. Sew a button in the middle.

STRIPES FROM RIPPED FABRIC

Quick and looks fantastic. Rip 2 inch (5 cm) wide strips from a linen fabric and sew the pieces together with a dense zigzag seam to make a piece big enough for the front of the cushion. Sew onto the front of the cushion with all the frayed seams visible and turned facing outward.

PATCHWORK WITH VISIBLE SEAMS

Felted jersey material, which can be found in craft stores, and old woolen sweaters that have been through a hot wash (thereby making them felted) can be cut and sewn without the edges fraying. This means all the seams can be turned outward and serve as decoration.

BACK AND FORTH

Crosses are simple and look really nice. Two strips of fabric laid one across the other make a decorative addition to the cushion. Sew with a "messy" stitch, with several overlapping stitches. Make them slightly too long and have them slip outside the motif to make it even more rugged.

SCRUNCHED STRIPS

A double ruffle running across the cushion is sometimes all that is needed. It looks especially nice on a long cushion. Make a strip from linen fabric, about 6 inches (15 cm) wide and at least twice the length of the pillow.

Draw a pencil line along the center of the strip. Use an extra strong thread and sew two gathering seams (use stitch length 5 and make the top tension slightly looser) on each side of the centerline, keeping a distance of approximately ⅝" from the centerline. Pull the thread on the wrong side to gather the wrinkles of the ruffle. Pin (or baste) the ruffle on the frontpiece of the cushion, adjusting the gathers evenly along the ruffle.

Attach the ruffle by topstitching twice, stitching close to each row of gathering stitches.

Remove the gathering stitches.

Tick Tock . . . Time Is Precious

Clocks make great decorations as well as having been proven useful for keeping track of the time. It's not difficult to make your own clock, so in no time at all you'll be placing clocks all over your home!

CLOCKWORK & HANDS

Simple mini quartz mechanisms can be found in craft stores. You choose mechanisms based on how thick the clockface is—anything from ⅛ to ¾ inch (2-18 mm). They come with rubber washers that can be used as buffers if required. Make sure you buy hands for the clock fitted to your chosen mechanisms, as they may vary slightly between brands.

To assemble the clock you need to drill a hole, 10 mm in diameter. The mechanism is placed on the back of the clock, using rubber washers if required, and then secured with a mounting nut on the front. Secure the hands in place.

PAPER CLOCK

With a piece of paper! That's how simple it is to make a clock in any pattern and color you like. Buy some thick scrapbooking paper and decorate it any way you want with words, numbers, pictures, labels. . . . Fold the paper in half, twice, and then unfold it. Make a hole in the middle and mount the clockwork. Attach to the wall using nails.

TIME FLIES

A small drawer placed upright on its edge can be transformed into a clock with a nostalgic feel. The clockwork is hidden inside the drawer proper. The front of the drawer has retained its little handle and worn, brown veneer, while the rest of the drawer has been painted white and adorned with painted numbers. It proudly displays the text *Tempus fugit*, "time flies," in Latin. Sand it down to get that old-fashioned, worn appearance, and mount the clockwork.

BOOK SOME TIME

An old book with a stiff, ornate cover can make a lovely shabby chic clock. Brush the cover with a dab of white paint. Paint with a light touch so the color doesn't quite cover it. Book covers can also be decorated with words, pictures, lace, or anything else that will enhance the look. Drill a hole in the front of the book to mount the clockwork. Use an X-Acto knife to cut a hole in the pages of the book, large enough to hide the clockwork inside the book itself.

Fancy Dressing

Mix and match
different patterns
to create a unique
piece of furniture
entirely covered in
fabric.

NEW CLOTHES

Unleash your creativity! Cut and paste, and mix and match colors and patterns. Thin fabric and glue can transform a boring piece of furniture into something extraordinary, and you'll have fun making it so.

The thinner and finer your fabric is, the easier it is to shape and smooth. Calico—thin fabrics designed for patchwork—can be found in craft and fabric stores. They are tightly and finely woven and can be cut into smaller pieces and strips. If the fabric has a busy pattern, the cuts and joints won't show.

MATERIAL

- A good-quality piece of second-hand furniture
- Calico—thin cotton fabric
- Denatured alcohol
- Fine sandpaper
- Mod Podge Hard Coat
- Clear acrylic varnish

HOW TO

1. Use a decent piece of furniture to avoid having to do too much prepwork. All you should have to do is rough up the surface with some fine sandpaper and then wipe it so it is dust free with some denatured alcohol.

2. Brush Mod Podge straight onto the furniture.

3. Place the cotton fabric onto the furniture and smooth down with your fingers.

4. Trim off any excess fabric so it can be applied smoothly without any creases or unnecessary bulk. Make small clips or cut out notches in the fabric in order to shape it smooth onto the surface.

5. Brush Mod Podge on top of the fabric, as the glue will harden the surface. When the first layer of glue has dried, you can brush on yet another coating or two of glue. Allow it to dry. The fabric is then protected by enough layers so you can rub the surface with fine sandpaper to give the surface a nicer finish.

6. Finish the piece by giving it a protective coating. Mod Podge Hard Coat can be used for this too, but if it's a surface that will get a lot of wear and tear, clear varnish is a better choice.

Fun and Colorful

Clear green, sunny yellow, tangy orange, bright pink, vibrant turquoise... These colors stand out like big exclamation points in light, white surroundings. Busy patterns and sassy colors with a hint of '70s groove find their way into country charm.

CONTRAST

Clear, bright colors contrast beautifully with really rough edges. This table has been used as a work surface, and the old planks of the table top bear the scars of many years' worth of use.

Terrible, horrible, silly seventies! We overdid the browns, greens, and oranges, the corduroy, the sauna yellow wooden panelling, and pop art patterns. Then we put it behind us with a shudder and vowed "never again!"

Now, however, enough time has passed for us to smile fondly at the clear colors, the shapes, and the crazy fabric and wallpaper patterns that we remember from our childhood. Though the wooden paneling of yellowed pine still makes me shudder.

Perhaps retro styles are better the second time around, because its trendiness gives us yet more choice. With a bit of distance, we can choose our favorite parts and hold dear the aspects that really speak to us. Not only that, we can use this era as inspiration, reinterpreting it and making it our own.

There might be some who protest and say that the style from the vibrant and sometimes crazy '70s hasn't got much to offer those who prefer a light and serene country style. However, we live in generous times that applaud individuality and encourage personalization, and a few splashes of color can be the icing on the cake to complement an all-white home. No interior decoration has to be permanent, and a few key splashes of color in otherwise neutral surroundings can work wonders when you simply fancy a change or need a bit of cheering up.

It's not always easy to get the style just right. Some styles easily blend with the country look without too much effort but this calls for a bit of a balancing act and there is no simple formula. Although a few suggestions won't hurt, remember to trust your instincts no matter what.

COLOR SPLASHES ON WHITE CANVAS

While some people claim that entirely white homes are boring, white homes can become a giant canvas—and you hold the brush. With minimal effort, your white home can take on whatever look you want. With furniture and textiles you can create different moods in the same room.

Josefine and Andreas's home is constantly changing. When they renovated their old house they gave it a light base. The ceiling and walls were covered with wooden panels and were painted white, just like the old wooden floors that were sanded down and painted white or light gray. The wood gives their home a warm and cozy feeling even when it is painted.

The possibilities are endless; it may start out romantic, but then change into a tough, industrial look. Other times it may be fun and vibrant, with color splashes giving attitude to all that white. This home is never boring. Not much work is needed for the bright colors to jump out at you like exclamation points against the white, and it changes the entire aesthetic of the room. Look into the kitchen; a yellow stool, a yellow hanging lamp, a table with orange legs, and a few pieces of turquoise bric-a-brac. Makes you smile, doesn't it?

A green thread

The grass green metal locker has a strong presence in the hall. The effect is enhanced by the green chair and the green striped bags. It really is this simple to repeat a color scheme and pull a room together to give a coherent feel. Above it all, a bright orange "farmer's heat lamp" hovers. Green + orange = seventies-era colors with a modern twist.

Clean and sparse

"You can't see the forest for the trees" is an expression that probably fits many homes. So many pieces jostle for space in our homes without us thinking about it. Start by clearing out and simplifying! The secrets behind those stylish photos in interior decorating magazines can be as easy as simply sorting through your belongings and clearing out (some of them).

With a bit of space opened up, your interiors will look completely different. The table is made from heavy planks laid across a frame of pipes that have been welded together. These are industrial pipes, used in the building of homes. Around this, Josefine and Andreas have placed assorted chairs—a mishmash of old and new, tarnished steel varieties, and kitchen stools with granny-style crocheted covers.

MIX PATTERNS AND STYLES <small>(PHOTO ON PREVIOUS PAGE)</small>

"Anything goes!" A fun and playful mix requires the courage to test out new things and not to be afraid to break a rule or two. With just a little fabric and only a splash of paint to add a hint of color to your furniture, the price tag won't be too high, and the biggest catastrophe you might have to face is that it might not come out quite the right shade or be the perfect match. That, however, is quickly repaired with another coat of paint or new cover.

The couch is made from a spring mattress on a base made of pallets. The couch got a cover made of stripy fabric and lots of cushions in bright colors and patterns. Grayed, weather-worn wood gives it an edge. We added an old-fashioned coffee table from the '40s with some new color to make a fun contrast. The cherry on top is the glamorous lamp with the shiny mother of pearl coins. This crazy combination only works because the surroundings (walls, ceiling, and floor) don't impose; rather, they help to enhance the decorations.

PAINT MORE

Imagine how much happiness can be found in a single can of paint. Buy a quart of your favorite color and repaint a few select items around the house. If you want a '70s feel, the color should be solid. It can be monochrome and combined with a patina or painted in a slightly worn style but using a bright color (instructions can be found on page 63).

WONDERFUL WINDOWS

A window in a wall between two rooms gives the feeling of light and openness and is a popular trick in shabby chic homes. If you're bold, paint the window frame in a color that pops; this makes the window a piece of art in its own right.

Crochet a Granny Square

Take a trip down memory lane and crochet a granny square. This is a great way to make a cute and fashionable piece for interior design with only your old, leftover yarn. When you have finished this challenge, try a granny's rose or aunty's flower square.

CHAIN STITCH, DOUBLE CROCHET, AND LOOP

Crocheting has come out of the old lady closet and has become become trendy once again. It's so helpful to those who enjoy having something to do with their hands. A few balls of yarn and a crochet hook makes the commute to work a time for some calm creativity. It's fun to try different color combinations, and the crazier the mix of colors, the better the result. You can mix different brands of yarn as long as you pick the same type (wool, cotton, or acrylic) and the same thickness.

It is easier to crochet if the yarn doesn't get too compact and hard, so use crochet hook 6 or 7 for yarns that recommend size 4/E.

If you're constantly changing color, you will have a lot of threads to secure, so be creative where you can and re-crochet the thread that you have just finished so that you attach it while you crochet. Or, you can have a sewing needle on hand and can secure all the threads as and when you finish each square. This leaves you with the fun stuff at the end—crocheting all the squares together into an even bigger piece.

GLOSSARY
ch = chain stitch
sl st = slip stitch
sc = single crochet
dc = double crochet
tr = triple crochet
chain stitch loop
loop

BUSY BEE BLANKET

In the olden days, lengthy crochet projects were the norm, but these days it's less common to crochet an entire blanket, unless it's baby sized. It does require some patience to make enough squares, but once you start with one and realize how much fun it is, you make another and another and on and on. In the lovely blanket on the previous page, the squares have been crocheted together on the diagonal to make a big piece.

SITTING PRETTY
Start with a good sized project and crochet little squares that can be combined into a cushion or a stool cover.

THE CLASSIC GRANNY SQUARE

Use as many colors as you want and crochet and build as many rounds as you want. A classic option is to use black or white as the main color on the outer-most round.

Cast on 6 ch and make into a ring with one sl st in the first ch.

Round 1: 3 ch, 2 dc around the ring, *3 ch, 3 dc around the ring*—3 times, 3 ch. Finish off with a sl st in the third ch.

Round 2: Change color. Start in a ch loop. 3 ch, 2 dc—3 ch—3 dc around the ch loop, *1 ch, 3 dc—3 ch—3 dc around the next ch loop*—3 times, 1 ch. Finish off with a sl st in the third ch.

Round 3: Change color. Start in a ch loop with 3 ch. 3 ch, 2 dc*—3 ch*—3 dc around the ch loop, *1 ch, 3 dc around the loop with 1 ch, 1 ch, 3 dc*—3 ch*—3 dc around the loop with 3 dc*—3 times, 1 ch, 3 dc around the loop with 1 ch, 1 ch. Finish off with one sl st in the third ch.

It's as simple as that, and the same basic principles are applied the whole time, and with each round the square increases by 1 group of 3 double crochets on each side.

AUNTY'S FLOWER SQUARE

For each square: 3 colors + a main color
Cast on 5 ch with the first color and make a ring with a sl st in the first ch.

Round 1: 4 ch, 3 unfinished tr (wind the yarn twice around the hook, pull the hook through the ring and pull the yarn through. Pull the yarn through 2 loops, then through the next 2, but leave the treble crochet's last stitch on the hook), when the third tr is in place, finish off by crocheting the yarn through the top stitch on all three tr + ch and collect them into a group. This makes the tip of the leaf on the flower. *4 ch, leaves with 4 tr in a group**—7 times. 4 ch, 1 sl st at the tip of the first leaf.

Round 2: Color 2*—Start in a loop with a ch*—3 ch, 3 dc in the same ch loop * 4 dc in the next ch loop, 6 ch, 4 dc in the next ch loop**—3 times, 4 dc in the next ch loop, 6 ch, 1 sl st in the third ch.

Round 3: Color 3*—first dc = 3 ch, then crochet 1 dc in every dc on the last round. Round the corner of the square with 3 dc, 3 ch, 3 dc around the ch loop. Repeat to the end of the round and finish off with a sl st in the third ch on the first double crochet.

Round 4: Main color*—First dc = 3 ch, then crochet 1 dc in every dc on the last round. Round the corner of the square with 2 dc, 3 ch, 2 dc around the ch loop. Repeat to the end of the round and finish off with a sl st in the third ch on the first double crochet.

ch = chain

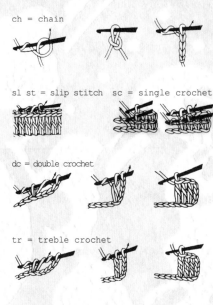

sl st = slip stitch   sc = single crochet

dc = double crochet

tr = treble crochet

Aunty's window square

Granny's rose square

AUNTY'S WINDOW SQUARE

For each square: 2 colors + main color

Cast on 6 ch on the first color and make a closed ring with a sl st in the first ch.

Round 1: 1 ch, 15 sc around the ring, finish off with a sl st in the first ch.

Round 2: 4 ch *9 ch, skip 3 sc, 1 dc in the next sc**—3 times, 9 ch, 1 sl st in the fourth ch.

Round 3: 1 ch, *11 sc around the sc loop, 1 sc in the dc* 3 times, 11 sc around the ch loop, 1 sl st in the first ch.

Round 4: 1 ch, 5 sc *1 sc, 3 ch, 1 sc (in the middle loop = the corner of the square), 11 sc**—3 times, 11 sc, finish off with a sc in the same stitch that you started with, 3 ch, and a sl st in the second ch.

Round 5: Change to the second color. Start in the ch loop at the corner of the square*—2 ch *13 sc, then 1 sc, 3 ch, 1 sc in the ch loop**—3 times, 13 sc, finish off with 1 sc in the same ch loop that you started in, 3 ch, and a sl st in the second ch.

Round 6: 2 ch, 14 sc, *1 sc, 3 ch, 1 sc in the ch loop, 15 sc**—3 times, 1 sc, 3 ch, 1 sc in the ch loop, finish off with a sl st in the second ch.

Round 7: Change to the main color*—start at the ch loop at the corner, 3 ch, 2 dc around the ch loop *skip 2 sc, 3 dc in the third sc*—5 times, skip 2 sc, 3 dc*—3 ch*—3 dc in the ch loop* 3 times. Skip 2 sc, 3 dc in the third sc*—5 times, skip 2 sc, 3 dc*—3 ch in the ch loop, finish off with a sl st in the third ch.

GRANNY'S ROSE SQUARE

For each square: Rose color, leaf color + main color.

Cast on 5 ch with the first color, close to a ring with a sl st in the first ch.

Round 1: Rose color *2 ch, 4 dc around the ring, 1 sl st around the ring**—4 times = the central petals of the rose.

Round 2: Add to the back of the first petals, 1 sl st in the back loop's third stitch, *keep the yarn at the back of the first round of petals, 4 ch, 1 sl st in the back loop of the third stitch in the next group**—3 times, 4 ch, 1 sl st in the first sl st.

Round 3: Make 1 sl st, 2 dc, 1 tc, 2 dc, 1 sl st around each ch loop.

Round 4: Change to the leaf color. On the back of the rose start with a sl st around the back loop, between two petals *6 ch, 1 sl st in the back loop between the petals**—4 times. Finish off with a sl st in the first sl st.

Round 5: 3 ch, 2 dc*—3 ch*—3 dc around the same ch loop *1 ch, 3 dc*—3 ch*—3 dc around the ch loop**—3 times, 1 ch, finish off with a sl st in the third ch.

Round 6: Change to the main color. 3 ch, 2 stitches*—3 ch*—3 dc in the same ch loop *1 ch, 3 dc around the loop of the first ch, 1 ch, 3 dc*—3 ch*—3 dc around the loop of 3 ch **—3 times, 1 ch, 3 dc around the loop of the ch, 1 ch. Finish off with a sl st in the third ch.

Round 7: 3 ch, 2 dc*—3 ch*—3 dc in the same ch loop, *1 ch, 3 dc around the loop of the first ch, twice, 1 ch, 3 dc*—3 ch*—3 dc around the loop of the 3 ch **—3 times, 1 ch, 3 dc around the loop of the first ch twice, 1 ch. Finish off with a sl in the third ch.

Round 8: 3 ch, 2 dc*—3 ch*—3 dc in the same ch loop, * 1 ch, 3 dc around the loop of the ch 3 times, 1 ch, 3 dc*—3 ch*—3 dc around the loop of the 3 ch **—4 times, 1 ch, 3 dc around the loop of the first ch 3 times, 1 ch. Finish off with a sl st in the third ch.

Shabby Freestyle

Hurry, hurry—this technique is a quick fix to turn an inexpensive piece of furniture into something with a little extra flair. Not suitable for those precious antiques, but it's a fun way to create a worn and slightly messy looking patina for when the urge to be creative hits you and you want quick results.

MELLOW YELLOW

A thrift store find for $10 and a splash of pretty color can be all it takes to brighten your day. A few bright pieces of furniture in an otherwise stark environment have a great effect and really catch the eye. A bright yellow table in a sober black and white bathroom works wonders!

PATINA

Messy and topsy turvy. If your end result looks like an old, colorful piece of furniture you just found, picked up, brought home, and put in place—then you've succeeded! If you're the type that tends to pay too much attention to detail and do very neat work, you can always pass the brush on to your kids and let them paint both the first and second coat!

Quick and clean

It's a lot easier to make a streaky, layered effect with a brush and get a patina look than trying to paint a perfectly smooth and even monochrome surface. Dare to give it a try and add a splash of color to your life!

MESSY PAINT

One of the hardest things to do is to paint a surface so it's perfectly smooth, shiny, and dust free in a solid color using gloss finish paint. Isn't it lucky then that we prefer the shabby, slightly worn look, full of charming little flaws? It's so is much easier to achieve!

MATERIAL

- An old piece of furniture or ornament
- A dull knife
- Paint Prep Cleaner, like T.S.P (trisodium phosphate liquid) or the more eco-friendly Citra Solv
- Fine sandpaper
- Water-based primer
- Water-based acrylic paint, low lustre/satin gloss for your choice of basic all-over color
- Water-based acrylic paint or hobby paint in different, contrasting colors
- A decent lacquer brush and a few cheap brushes
- A large flat brush

HOW TO

1. You don't need to make the piece you are going to paint perfectly smooth, nor fill any holes or cracks. In fact, just the opposite. Give it a good bashing with a heavy chain if it's too nice, smooth and brand-new looking. If some of the paint is peeling, just scrape it off, and if the edges and corners are damaged and feel sharp or pointy, just sand them down.

2. Dust off and then use T.S.P. to clean the whole piece—follow instructions on the container. Allow to dry.

3. Paint one coat of the primer and when this is dry paint a coat of your basic color, using slightly sloppy brush strokes for both coats. The color is meant to cover the surface, but you can brush back and forth and in a zigzag motion. You can even keep brushing the painted surface as the paint starts to dry as this is when the paint gets slightly sticky and the brush will leave even more obvious marks, giving the paint a streaky and animated structure. Allow to dry.

4. Paint the basic color in patches all over the surface. Add smaller patches in other colors (on the yellow base, I dotted small splotches of orange and bright pink and on the turquoise one, mint green and marine blue). Brush the paint so that everything blends together and allow to dry. If you don't like the effect in any one spot, you can just add a new color on top. Allow to dry.

5. To get a good effect, dry brush the surface. For this you need a tiny bit of color on a cheap flat brush (a cheap brush gives a streaky effect). The color should be in sharp contrast to the rest of the colors, preferably a black or dark brown to give a "dirty" effect and a bit of white to give the surface a soft, misty sheen. Dip the brush in the paint and pull it over some newspaper until it's almost dry. Using a light touch, wisp the brush here and there all over the surface to make sparse, streaky brush strokes back and forth. This gives your piece a patinated effect.

Letters
& Numbers XL

Do you love letters? Make them count! Both letters and numbers make great ornaments, and the larger they are the better the effect. So make your own; it's not difficult or expensive. Make several at a time and give them away as gifts.

SIZEABLE S

Play with patches of paper or thin fabric and cover the whole letter in myriad patterns and colors. I used a packet of ready-made origami paper, which gave me a whole bunch of both patterned and monochrome paper. I divided these into smaller squares and glued them close together, with the edges slightly overlapping. You can read more about Styrofoam lettering on pages 67–68.

Giants

Go big or go home! Make mega-sized letters to
hang on the wall or to lean nonchalantly
against the wall. The huge 2 in the photo is
covered with wallpaper, which gives it a
tough, durable surface.

K

If you saw letters out of
thick Styrofoam, you can
make them wide enough to
stand without support.
This letter has been
wrapped in tissue paper
that has been scrunched
onto the glue-covered
surface. This gives it a
great texture, even if the
letter itself is painted
entirely white.

XL

MATERIAL

- Sheet of Styrofoam (can be purchased at a hardware store in varying thicknesses)
- Wallpaper, tissue paper, gift wrap, or thin fabric
- Mod Podge
- Paint (optional)

TOOLS

- Coping saw/jigsaw
- Sandpaper
- Paint brush

The Styrofoam is covered because it's not only quite dull looking but also fragile.

HOW TO

1. First make a template. Draw a number on a piece of paper, freehand, and use a ruler for the straight parts. The easiest numbers are the ones that have an open shape. Numbers with holes in them, like an 8, are a bit trickier.

2. Draw the number/letter on the Styrofoam and then cut it out using a saw. A jigsaw is more effective but leaves more of a mess. A coping saw doesn't cost as much and has a fine, thin blade that gives a nice, finished edge. The surfaces don't need to be perfect, but any loose bits should be removed with sandpaper.

COVER WITH WHOLE PIECES OF PAPER OR FABRIC

3. Cut strips of paper/fabric, about 1 inch (3 cm) wider than the thickness of the Styrofoam. Liberally cover with Mod Podge on the wrong side of the paper or fabric. If you are using paper, leave it for a while to allow it to absorb the moisture. Attach the strip to the side of the Styrofoam and make small clips along the edge of the strip so that you can fold and smooth down the edge on the front- and back side of the letter/number. Allow to dry.

4. Place the number or letter on top of the wrong side of the paper/fabric and trace along the outlines. Cut out the piece from the paper or fabric, 2 mm less than your tracing line. Coat with Mod Podge on the wrong side, allow it to absorb. Then attach it to the Styrofoam. Allow to dry completely.

DRESS WITH PATCHWORK

5. For the edges of the Styrofoam, repeat stage 3 from the instructions. For the front and back of the number/letter, brush smaller patches of paper or fabric with Mod Podge and place flat against the surface. When it's dry, the paper hardens and becomes firm, meaning you can cut it with an X-Acto knife or box cutter along the edge of the number/letter. Fabric, on the other hand, is easier to cut as you go.

DRESS WITH TISSUE PAPER

6. The easiest! Brush the Mod Podge straight onto the Styrofoam. Scrunch some tissue paper and place on the glued surface so that the paper creates wrinkles and creases. Coat the silk paper with glue—use a brush to press it onto the surface and remove any air bubbles. At the same time, the glue works as a clear varnish, which stiffens the paper.

7. It's a bit arduous to cover the whole number in one go with scrunchy, messy paper, so do half at a time and let it dry in between.

PAINT!

8. Regardless of what you have covered your number with, you can cover it with paint once you are done gluing. You can either paint the whole piece or give it a bit of an edge by drybrushing it with a little bit of paint.

Industrial Finery

A slightly more hardened edge to country style! Vintage and shabby chic are made grittier with a more robust industrial vibe. Some aspects have long been loved by "countryphiles," so here we'll introduce a few tough twists to the otherwise light, romantic home. This makes an exciting and surprising blend to really enhance the look.

Make room for metal

Storage in industrial chic style is made with simple metal shelves. These can be found in hardware stores and companies that sell interiors to factories and other people in the industry. Place food and smaller items in glass or metal jars. Rattan or metal baskets and old wooden boxes provide practical decorations for the shelves.

"Nothing is wrong until you call it such."

We are already familiar with the rusted, worn, and battered. Gray, like concrete, zinc, tin, and silver are old favorites. Industrial vintage is a close relative of romantic country style, so why not combine the best of both worlds? It's appropriate to talk about "masculine" and "feminine" here, as industrial aesthetic has always been seen as more manly while the lightest lace, bows, and frills are seen as ladylike. But you don't really have to choose one or the other. A combination of the two can be just what it takes to create balance and harmony in your home—a sort of "industrial romance." Don't be afraid to mix sweet and sour, hard and soft, dull and shiny, sheer and robust . . . play with shapes and contrasts, and experiment. Nothing is wrong until you call it such.

A completely new side to industrial style that is worth trying is lacquered metal and blank metallic surfaces used in a way that isn't considered country style. Items don't have to be old but can be brand-spanking new, with a high-tech vibe!

AN INDUSTRIAL KITCHEN WITH A COUNTRY FEEL

Josefine and Andreas's kitchen has a modern feel to it: clean lines, stainless steel, and a shiny finish akin to a professional kitchen. In the wall over the kitchen sink they have placed a large window frame of rust-colored metal: a style that is reminiscent of old factories. However, we still see hints of cozy, country style with the porcelain sinks, wooden wall panels, wicker baskets, and the classic tiles.

A tap with 'tude
Strengthen the feeling of
a professional kitchen with
a cool, multifunctional
tap.

Fix it with a lamp

Metal lamps can easily clamp onto shelves, where they look cool and are easy to move around as needed.

Wicked wood

In a trendy, interior decorating store in London I spotted a shelf that had been designed and built to look like stacked fruit crates. However, the price tag indicated that this was far from a "cheap" option!

Save your money and make it original instead. If you want a scruffy style, scout out old wooden crates at thrift stores or yard sales, and find fruit boxes from the local fruit and vegetable market. Keep them as they are or stain them to make them slightly darker.

The coffee table is an old cable reel that has been painted and given wheels, and the lamp once served its function in a dentist's office. Lamps are a great way to update your home. Swap out lamps or move them around. It's easier than repainting every time you want a change!

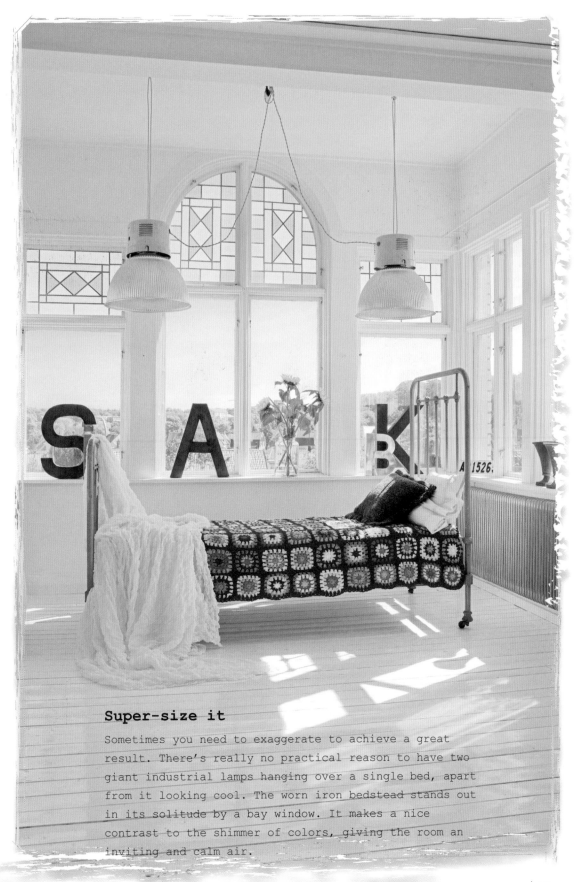

Super-size it

Sometimes you need to exaggerate to achieve a great
result. There's really no practical reason to have two
giant industrial lamps hanging over a single bed, apart
from it looking cool. The worn iron bedstead stands out
in its solitude by a bay window. It makes a nice
contrast to the shimmer of colors, giving the room an
inviting and calm air.

Male and female

Like a portrait of a lady with soft curves and a gentleman in a firm pose as if standing to attention, the divan and the metal cupboard complement each other and work better together than they would on their own. In other words, their placement here is a happy marriage and the theme is followed through with ruffled, romantic cushions, lamps, and metal lettering.

INSPIRING SPIRALS

If you want to achieve a really tough industrial look, shiny spiral duct tubes will do the trick. Just like Josefine did, you can add a fake air duct with no real function. In the right place, it can make an appropriately harsh addition to the edgier industrial style. Big clocks with straightforward numbers round out the look nicely, as do old-fashioned electric fans.

ASSEMBLY! ATTENTION!

Even the most common, everyday items can turn into fun and unusual ornaments when you line them up right. A single shaving brush doesn't cut it but a whole row of brushes standing at attention makes for a fun collection. Old signs are also great as extra detailing. They should really be originals with authentic dents and rust spots, but these days you can also buy a variety of newly manufactured signs for this purpose.

Gray and concrete

The raw texture of gray concrete definitely belongs in genuine industrial style. Additionally, gray is a color that can be paired with anything, either as untreated concrete or as paint. The concrete's hard, matte, and sometimes grainy surface stands out when placed in contrast with other textures and surfaces, such as crisp white, flowery and translucent, and soft, padded textiles. So instead of painting a newly polished surface, why not leave it as is, untreated!

Rustic and raw

Stairs made from floor plating? We kid you not. The seemingly ordinary wooden staircase has been covered in a rubber mat that looks like floor plate. The walls have been covered with robust pieces of wood and give a striped effect, as only every other panel is painted. Everything is tied together and looks great with the old-fashioned, leaded-glass window.

It might look harsh, but it's soft to the touch and easy to maintain. Covering the stairs might be a bit tricky if you're a novice, so get a professional to do it for you. A similar looking mat is manufactured by American Biltrite and is called "Mirra Metallic." Check out their site www.american-biltrite.com for a distributor near you.

Make It Metal

Imagine how much you can do with a dash of paint! With the help of a brush, boring bits of furniture and ornaments take on new personality with a metallic sheen, just as if they were really made of metal.

GALVANIZED HEADBOARD?

Who would have guessed that this funky headboard is particleboard in disguise? With some panels and a bit of color, it's transformed into a great headboard of metal sheeting without the coldness of real metal. Do some style clashing by making up the bed with lace, embroidery, and frills, or try a few colorful patterns.

PAINT METALLIC

MATERIAL

- Fine sandpaper
- Paint Prep Cleaner, like T.S.P (trisodium phosphate liquid)
- Wood glue
- Masking tape
- Molding ⅜ inch x 1 inch (8 x 27 mm) or ⅜ x 1.3 inches (8 x 33 mm)
- Angle molding as needed
- Wooden button plugs, 12 or 18 mm in diameter (found in craft stores)
- Small, cone-head nail, 1 x 12 mm
- Chalk, ground into a powder
- A good quality brush for applying the varnish
- A cheaper brush with sparse bristles

PAINT

- Primer for wood, water-based Matte Metallic Paint from Modern Masters (www.modernmasters.com) will do the job, but you can also ask your local paint store for similar options.
- Matte Metallic Paint / Pewter—1 quart for base coat and effect painting
- Matte Metallic Paint / Platinum-Silver—for effect painting

HOW TO

1. Prepare the surface that is to be painted as needed; sand it down to a dull finish and wash down with a product such as TSP. Larger damage should be fixed but small bumps and scratches can be left.

2. The molding can be glued to the surface if you want raised "panels" on the faux-metal. Glue the button plugs onto the molding. Let the glue dry and then reinforce the glue by adding a tiny cone-headed nail into every button. The nail is so small you may need a pair of pliers to hold it.

3. If you prefer, you can skip the molding and glue the buttons straight onto the smooth surface. Draw a straight line with a pencil to help you place the buttons in a straight line. Now, use paint to create the effect of metal slats.

4. Prime your surface with one coat. Then use the Metallic Pewter as base coat on the surface. Don't bother being neat—instead paint messily for better effect. Drag the brush back and forth, making sure the whole surface is covered. Let it dry and, if needed, paint another coat in the pewter shade to make sure it's completely covered.

5. Paint the surface once using the dark gray metallic color. To create a more exciting surface with some texture, sprinkle some chalk onto the painted surface. Paint over this, blending the chalk and the color, giving you a slightly raised effect on the surface.

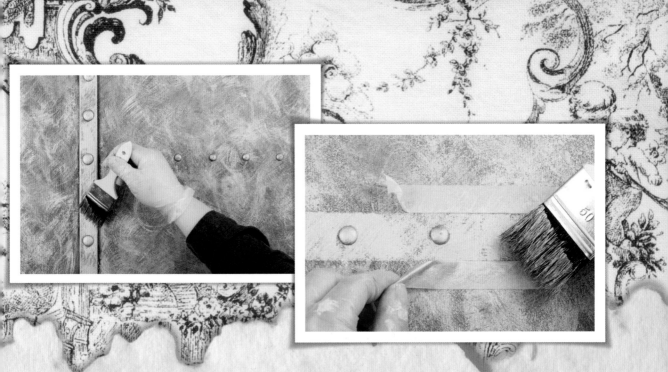

6. To create the effect of metal that has been brushed and polished by an angle grinder, the light silver color should be brushed on with the sparse-bristled brush in several thin layers. Pour a splash of paint onto a paper plate and dip the brush's outer edge in the color; pull the brush over the rim of the plate so that you just have a tiny amount of paint on the brush. Using a very light hand, brush over the surface so you get a streaky, sparse effect. The first time, brush in a criss-cross shape across the surface.

7. The second time, add the silver paint using small circles; the third time, make crosses again. In this way you slowly build up a surface that looks like brushed metal. On the final coat, you can just brush the "slatted" bit.

8. If you haven't used molding to make slats, you can paint on a slatted effect instead. For this, the surface must be completely dry and cured for at least 24 hours. Place masking tape on each side of the rows of glued on "bolts." Don't press the tape too hard, as you risk removing some paint when you take the tape off. Paint the slats extra silvery by lightly brushing the surface a few times. Remove the tape and allow the paint to dry completely.

9. When the paint is completely dry, place masking tape along the silver colored "slatting" and then brush the dark gray metal paint lightly along the tape. Just a touch will give the illusion of a shadow along the slat. The slat now looks like it's a raised surface.

10. To finish, protect the surface with one or two coats of clear varnish. Use a water-based crystal clear acrylic varnish that doesn't turn yellow.

Metal furniture

If you plan to buff and paint your wooden furniture
to look like metal, it needs to have a flat and
smooth surface. There is no place for anything
curved and embellished. Plain, linear furniture, on
the other hand, is perfect!

Starry Eyed

Why be shy when it comes to decorating? Go big! An XL sized three dimensional star takes center stage and is guaranteed to catch the eye. What's even better is when you tell people you made it yourself.

MAKE A STAR

This calls for a bit of extra work, but you don't need any special tools to make it. To give it that extra shine, I painted my star as if it were made from slatted and dented metal, though it's really made from cardboard, duct tape, and wire thread.

XL STAR

MATERIAL
- 2 sheets of stiff, white cardboard, 27 x 40 inches (70 x 100 cm), 2 mm thick
- Masonite (optional)
- Silver tape
- Wire thread

TOOLS
- X-Acto knife or carpet knife
- Steel ruler
- Scissors
- Drill

HOW TO

1. Draw the templates from page 86 at full size on a piece of heavy duty paper. Using the templates, draw five points and one spine onto the stiff cardboard. If possible, saw the spine from a piece of masonite, as it will be more durable. Place the cardboard on a non-delicate surface, preferably a thick piece of glass, and cut out the parts for the star.

2. Follow the instructions on page 83 and put together the 5 points of the star, edges against each other. Tape the parts together using duct tape across the joints; this forms the front of the star. Leave a gap between the two outer edges, which will overlap slightly. Flip the star and face the backside upwards. Tape along the centerline of each point to give it some extra strength.

3. Flip the star to be front facing again and make an incision along the centerline of each point (see the lined markings) so that you can easily fold the point in an upturned fold by bending the cardboard along the incision.

4. When all the five points of the star have been folded, tape the last remaining edges on the front of the star shut. This will force the shape of the star to raise and become 3D.

Decorate your star!
You can paint it or
dress it with decou-
page. If the paint
doesn't want to stay
on the shiny surface
of the silver tape,
take some denatured
alcohol to a rag and
wipe the surface of
the tape to give the
paint a better grip.

5. Without support the star won't keep its shape, which is why you need the spine. Drill two small holes on each side of the taped joints. Thread some wire around the star; the wire needs to go across each edge on the back and across the joint between the two holes on the front.

6. Pull the wire so that the star keeps its three-dimensional shape. Place the spine against the back of the star and, with the help of the wire, hook the star onto the spine's edges. Twist the wire ends together.

7. Make the star more durable by adding silver tape along the middle fold of each of the edges. Also add tape across the edge's tip and fold the tape in towards the back of the star.

The star's edge

The star's backbone

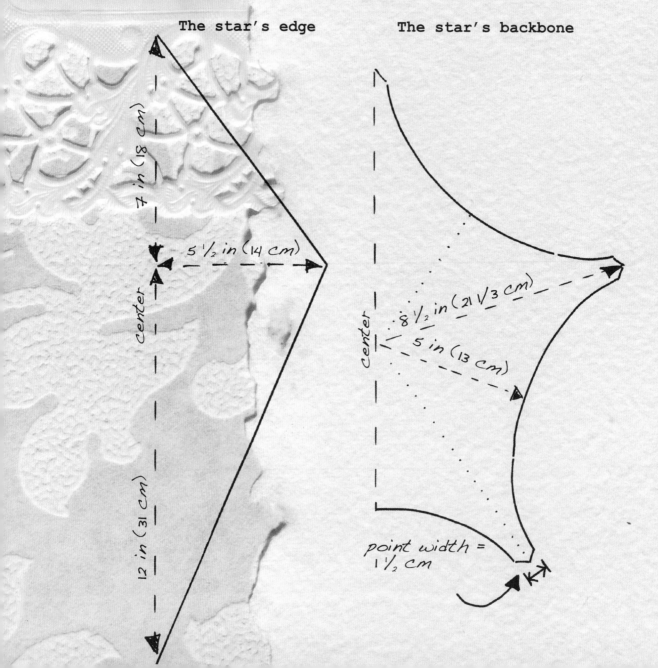

7 in (18 cm)

5 ½ in (14 cm)

center

12 in (31 cm)

center

8 ½ in (21 √3 cm)

5 in (13 cm)

point width = 1 ½ cm

A Cheeky Chalkboard

A door from before

If you live in a more modern house or an apartment, an old door can help create a more rustic feel. Use the door as a piece of furniture and lean it against the wall. If it's slightly worn and scuffed then all the better!

On this door, the panels were painted over with chalkboard paint and placed in the hall as a fun piece of furniture that doubles up as a space for messages and reminders. In addition, it's perfect for hanging other decorative items, as a few nails hammered into an already worn door won't make a big difference.

Black chalkboard paint with white chalk makes for an interesting aesthetic that fits not only with the romantic country style, but also with the slightly more robust industrial style; it works with anything!

PERFECT POTS

If, like me, you have a cupboard full of flower pots that you don't know what to do with, you can paint them black and make them look a lot more interesting. Planting new seeds or replanting old plants becomes a lot more fun when you can write on the black paint. Small pots can be used to decorate a table or as place cards. Write the guest's name on the pot and place them on the table.

HOW TO

Wash and scrub the pots clean using a little bit of detergent and a dash of denatured alcohol in the water.

Dry thoroughly.

The chalkboard paint adheres very well to terracotta and other matte surfaces. However, cover the inside of the pot with a few coats of water-based clear varnish so that the damp doesn't penetrate through the pot. The pots in the upper photo have been decorated with strips of paper that have been glued around the edge using Mod Podge.

To the bargain basement

Walk around a thrift store and check out the section that offers old wooden items. There's no telling how many items can be made into cute decorations with a little bit of chalkboard paint. Not only can you write on them with a bit of chalk, but you can also create lovely patterns. For example, you could write a comment on the fruit one week ("Bananas are great!"), draw chalk stripes on the bowl another, spots the following . . . the only limit is your imagination!

Globally

A sense of adventure, a love of travel, and a taste for maps and globes are very trendy. It doesn't matter if the borders are no longer accurate on older globes; you can still use them to decorate. As a reminder of how infinitely small we are on this planet, I painted mine black, except for my little mother country of Sweden. It can be tricky to get paint to adhere to a plastic surface, but if you lightly sand the globe with some fine sandpaper and wash it with some TSP, it will work wonders. Here, I've written a thought in Swedish.

Tray text

Repaint a basic wooden tray with chalkboard paint and you get double the usage. You can use it for serving, and even write the menu on it! When it is not in use, lean it against the wall or hang it on a hook and write messages on it.

Rope Tricks

Hemp, sisal, coconut—ropes are great props. They feel robust and natural, so why not tie them into some of your home décor?

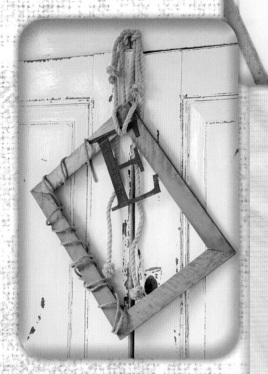

Tangled up

Use chunky ropes and heavy duty string to hang ornaments or pictures on the wall. It makes a cool detail that can be decorative just on its own. An empty frame with a letter tangled in rope becomes a work of art in itself.

A wreath of coconut and hemp

Wind, wrap, and tangle! Rope and string in varying sizes make great-looking wreaths. Use a base made of straw or wind a thin base from wire. Then you can experiment with the rope and string you already have on hand. A glue gun to secure the ends is always good too.

Tantalizing tangles

Thick ropes all in a tangle
look solid just the way
they are, so you don't need
to do anything with them.
Just leave them out in a
basket or hang a bunch of
rope on a wall hook. It
doesn't get simpler than
this.

A robust lamp cord

Give your lamp a bit of
attitude and make the
fixture decorative! Thin
electrical cords can be
hidden using a thick rope.

HOW TO

1. Use thick rope, at least 1 inch (2 cm) in diameter, that is tightly twisted together. You need two lengths that are slightly longer than the cord or lead you are planning to wrap. One rope is made from three lengths that in turn consist of several thin strands twined together.

2. Carefully undo the twining of one of the ropes without ruining the twisted shape of the rope. The cord will take up a bit of space and you won't be able to get the rope to cover it completely. Therefore you need to separate the other length of rope and use one of the strands from this.

3. Place the four corkscrew-shaped pieces of rope around one end of the cord and attach by winding some thin wire around it. Then "retwine" the rope while at the same time merging the cord into the center of the rope.

4. Tidy up the beginning and end of the ropehanger with a tuft, which can be made from the remaining rope. Separate all the threads from the rope and cut into 4 inch (10 cm) lengths. Collect them into a tuft around the ends of the rope and attach by winding a thin piece of string around them.

A Little Less Than Perfect

It feels like just the right amount of work. Raw and rough wooden pieces marked by time and a bit worn. Setting things askew is not only the right fit for today's fashion, but it's also pretty easy to do!

Whether you like it or not, things often end up a little less than perfect. So why not pretend that was your intention all along?

If your entire home consisted of old wooden boxes stacked on top of each other, shabby furniture, and ornaments hammered together from recycled bits of wood, and if you couldn't shut a single cupboard door and all the chairs wobbled, . . . well, you would probably think your talents don't lie in decorating. This concept relies on contrasts, a mix of old and new, and this is what makes it just right.

NOW & THEN

In Josefine and Andreas's family room we see a prime example of how opposites attract. New and shiny and high-tech, versus worn, shabby, and recycled can make for an interesting combination.

They needed a new TV stand but didn't like any of the new ones they found. Luckily, they found a pile of wooden pallets, which meant free wood. Could it be so hard to make their own TV stand? It was a great success and they ended up with the coolest TV stand in the neighborhood, for only the cost of a few nails and screws. And if the whole project had been a catastrophe, it wouldn't have mattered. The failed experiment would have just fueled a barbeque or a bonfire instead. Using old pieces rescued from the garbage makes it okay to create small disasters. Trying is learning by doing and the worst that can happen is that we're given the opportunity to try again.

COOL CONTRASTS

It should be weather worn and graying, with holes and cracks in the wood, preferably so worn that it looks like driftwood. In this case, a pallet is the best. Give it some TLC and wipe some oil over the old, dry wood. Painting it can be hard, as you can't always get into all the nooks and crannies.

In Andreas and Josefine's home, the corner couch has been built with a base made from pallets. You can hardly see them as they are covered by sheepskins and mattresses, but under all this there is another detail; the shiny new factory-fresh wheels. The metallic industrial style is a great contrast to the old wood.

SUPER SIGNS

Interiors made from recycled wood aren't always about furniture. It can just as well be a single, fun item that is there just to look pretty. When you suddenly get an urge to be creative, projects that can be made in an hour are great, and are even better when you can update your home without spending more than a bit of imagination and elbow grease.

Take a walk around. What can you find behind the garage? Or down in the cellar? An odd oar, a few pieces of wood, and a handful of nails gave Josefine a really funky looking sign.

Breathe New Life into Old Pallets

"Driftwood" is a term that evokes a sense of the sea, wind, salty waves lapping against soft sand, adventures, and a touch of mystery. "A pallet" doesn't have quite the same ring to it, but if you don't live close to a windswept beach, the likelihood of finding enough driftwood to build with is minimal. In this case, old, worn pallets work just as well.

A MAGICAL FLOOR CLOCK

Marvelously excessive! If you just want to keep track of time, there are much simpler ways to do so, but I love the clock made from worn wooden planks modeled after a grandfather clock.

Material

- 2 furring strips, 1 inch x 2 inches x 8 feet, cut to 75" (190 cm) long with slight angle on each end
- Pallet wood, 16 inches (40 cm) long, preferably all approx. the same thickness but with varying widths
- 1 clock mechanism to fit a clockface of ¾ inch thickness
- Hands for the clock mechanism
- Wood screws, flat head, 1½ inches (40 mm) long
- Fine nails, approx. 1½ inches in diameter and 1½ inches long
- Wood glue

Tools

- Sander
- Jigsaw
- Power drill, drill and driver bits
- Mitre saw

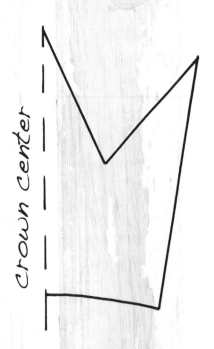

Crown Center

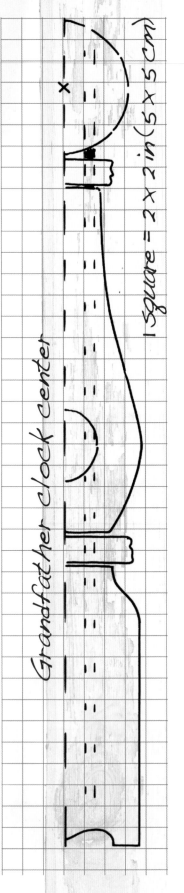

Grandfather clock center

1 square = 2 x 2 in (5 x 5 cm)

1 square

HOW TO

1. Cut the furring strips to a total length of 75 inches, with a slight angle at each end. Polish with a bit of sandpaper and paint in a neutral gray tone.

2. The palletwood should be sanded down at the front and lengthways along the edges. Place the palletwood one after the other with a distance of approx. $^3/_8$ inch (1 cm) between them, backsides facing up, to a total length of 65 inches. Glue the furring strips along the middle of the palletwood, parallel to each other. When the glue starts to set, predrill pilot holes for the screws to stop the wood from splitting. Then, strengthen the whole piece by adding the wood screws along the furring strips.

3. Spread out a big sheet of paper to make a template for the body of your clock. You may need to change the shape and adapt it to fit the width of your wooden boards. Draw the shape of the clock onto the front of the boards and cut out using a jigsaw. Carve, hack, and chip away along the short ends of the boards, then sand down and shape.

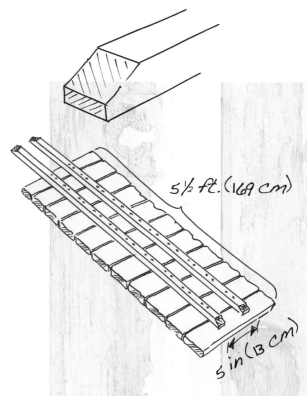

5½ ft. (169 cm)

5 in (13 cm)

THE CLOCK FACE

4. Make a round paper template, 12 inches (31 cm) in diameter. Place four palletwood boards on a flat surface with about a $^1/_8$–$^2/_8$ inches gap between them. Trace the contour of the template and saw the boards to a round shape. Sand the edges and then attach to the remaining stretch of the furring strips, using glue and screws to make the clock face. Drill a hole, (10 mm) in diameter, in the center of the clock face.

5. You can adorn the body of the clock with pieces of pallet wood or real driftwood, which can be glued and nailed on top of the two horizontal boards making them look like molding, glass covers, and any other detailing you might find on a standing clock, giving it a three-dimensional effect.

6. Crowning glory. The base of the crown should be gently curved to follow the contour of the clock face. Use the paper template for the clock face when you draw the outlines of the crown onto the wood to give you the correct shape. Saw out the crown using a jigsaw, chip at the edges with a knife, and then sand down.

7. Drill two holes, $^1/_{12}$" in diameter, with 2 inches (5 cm) between them, in both the crown and the edge of the clock face. Remove the head of the nail and tap into the hole in the crown. Attach the crown onto the clock face using glue.

TIP

If you want to paint some unique decorations on the chair, such as words in a fancy lettering, make sure to do this before the wooden panels are in place. This allows you to do your work comfortably at a table, one panel at a time, and if it doesn't turn out the way you wanted, you can easily make a new panel or sand it down and start again.

PALLET FLAIR IN A SHABBY CHAIR

Chairs are both decorative and useful to have, whether it's a solitary chair indoors, or several placed outside to create a restful seating area.

MATERIAL (ALL MEASUREMENTS COME IN INCHES)

- Planed pine—2 pieces measuring 2" x 6" x 8 ft (weathershield for outdoor use)
- Palletwood—10 pieces around $3/4$" x 2-$15/16$" x 18-$1/8$"
- Crosspieces—board 1 x 2 inches—2 lengths 14 inches
- Nuts, bolts, and washers—2 x #12 or #14, 4 inches
- Finishing nails or ovalhead screws, approx 1 $5/8$" long
- Wood glue

TOOLS

- Jigsaw
- Sander
- Power drill, drill and driver bits
- Hammer

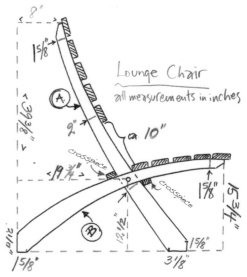

HOW TO

1. Draw templates in heavy duty paper for A—the back support/ front legs and B—seat support/back legs to full scale. Saw out two A-pieces and two B-pieces from the heavy wood, prefera- bly with a band saw to give you better precision, but a jigsaw also works. Drill holes in all four parts for the nuts and bolts, a smidgen larger than the diameter of the bolt.

2. Sand down the pieces that make the chair frame. If you plan to use it outside, place the parts in an empty paint tin with oil to impregnate it, leaving it 24 hours to allow the wood to soak up the oil until it is saturated. Paint the A and B parts as well as the crosspieces so that they are completely finished, before as- sembling the chair.

3. Assemble parts A and B in pairs using the nuts and bolts. Pull the nuts fast and position legs according to the measurements in the drawings. Prepare the horizontal crosspieces by predrilling pilot holes for the screws, close to the short ends (this is to prevent the wood from splitting). Place the crosspieces as the drawing shows, thus locking the crossed legs into position. Secure the crosspieces in place with screws. Fasten the nuts as tightly as you can.

4. The seat and back from the old pallets are sawn, sanded, and painted so that they are completely finished before you mount them onto the frame of the chair. The easiest way to do this, is to first attach the seating panels, evenly spaced, with some glue. When the glue has dried, secure the wood panels in place using nails or screws. Drill holes first to stop the wood from splitting. Fold the chair over and place it with the back up and repeat with the back panels.

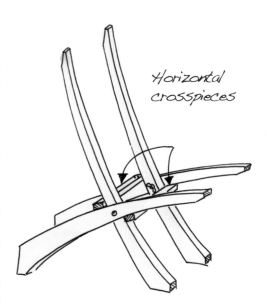

Horizontal crosspieces

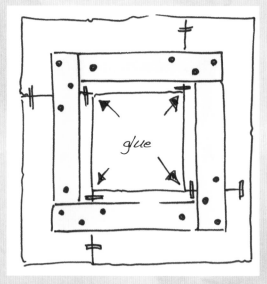

Material

- Old wood
- Wood glue
- ¾ inch wood screws
- Molding, ¼" x 1 ³⁄₈"

RUSTIC FRAMES

Solid, slightly graying frames look great with new black and white photographs, but even better with really old ones! A serious looking gentleman in his Sunday best or beautiful ladies from the turn of the century, dressed in lace, are a great fit with the antique-looking, worn frames.

HOW TO

1. The great news is that you don't need any advanced equipment to make these. A decent mitre saw, a sturdy staple gun, and a power drill is enough. Chop the old wood at a 90 degree angle in four equal lengths. Place on a flat surface, backsides up. Dab some glue on the cut ends and press together to create the frame. A few staples from the staple gun will keep the frame in place.

2. Draw a line around the frame, about ½ inch (1.5 cm) from the picture opening in the center of the frame. Measure the line and add 1³⁄₈ inches—that gives you the length of the molding. Cut for lengths of molding. Dab some glue on the molding's flat side and attach around the opening of the center of the frame. The molding should go across the joints of the frame to strengthen and steady the structure of the frame further.

3. Drill pilot holes for the screws in the molding to prevent it from splitting and then add some small screws to secure the glue.

Solen sjunker långsamt ned bak skogen, herrlig är de rika färgers prakt! Hvarje buske är … spunnen, hvarje li…

Hör, o hör, de silfverklara to… Kärleks fröjd och kval hor i … Himlens …

… aftonstund

BIRDHOUSE

Don't worry—these birdhouses won't fill up with uninvited feathered tennants—they're only meant to look good. Several of these birdhouses lined up in a row looks charming, so why not make more than one?

MATERIAL

- 4 lengths of rough palletwood, about 3 in (75 mm) wide, 8–12 inches (20–30 cm) in length
- 2 lengths of rough palletwood, about 3 in (75 mm) wide, 6 inches (15 cm) in length
- Wooden stick, around ¼ inches in diameter, 1½–2 inches (4–5 cm) in length
- Finishing nails, about 1⅓ inches –1⅔ in (35–40 mm) long
- Wood glue

HOW TO

1. Cut the palletwood for the side A of the birdhouse into shape, lengthwise, to make it ½ inch (1 cm) more narrow so they are 65 mm wide. Glue the wood together following the illustration's instructions, and strengthen the glue using nails. Don't use nails more than halfway along the length, from bottom edge and up, as you still need to saw the shape of the bird house.

2. Cut the pointy gable shape of the birdhouse using a mitre saw. Drill a bigger hole, about 1 inch (25 mm) in diameter, 1½–2 inches (4–5 cm) down from the tip of the house. Drill a smaller hole, ¼ inch in diameter, about 1½ inches (3½ cm) below the larger hole.

3. The lower short end of the roof is cut at a 45 degree angle. Cut the parts for the roof into the correct lengths with a straight edge, part A = 4 inches (11 cm), part B = 4 ⅞ inches (13 cm). Glue and nail part B to the short side of part A.

4. Glue and nail the roof onto the birdhouse so that the roof juts out around ½ inch (1 cm) on the front. The back is flat.

5. The little stick can be adjusted as required using a knife and is glued into the smaller hole.

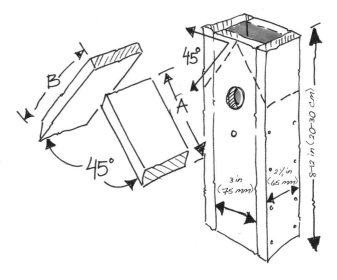

TIPS

* Pallets are worth good money and if they're the more durable variety, they are usually intended to be recycled back to their original purpose: storage and shipping. This means that you will need to ask permission before taking any pallets you may find, or else it's considered theft.
* Pallets do, however, have a finite lifespan and when they have been used a few times and gotten knocked around a bit, they'll get discarded. These pallets have the exact kind of vintage feel we're looking for, and usually you can get them for free before they are thrown out.
* Sharp wood can be dangerous and rough surfaces collect dust that is impossible to wipe away. However, you can easily fix this without losing the charm of the wood. Old forgotten nails and gravel embedded in the pallets make using a planer or a band saw an absolute no-no. Because of this, you'll need to do this work by hand with powertools—it's easier and cheaper to replace sawblades in a jigsaw!

HOW TO

1. Use a jigsaw to cut the planks on the pallet to get the longest bits possible without any nails.
2. If you want to enhance the appearance of driftwood, you can notch the plank a little along the edges and short ends, by simply sawing in a jagged manner. Making a few deep grooves with a knife also gives character.
3. Sand down with a sander and a medium grit sandpaper. The sanding won't make the planks "as new"; rather, they will still be rough around the edges. Just sand down the worst of the roughness to remove any sharp splinters, if you're making decorative items, or to make the surface soft and smooth if you're making items to use as furniture—no one wants a splinter in their bottom!
4. You can acheive a more gray or a deeper shade in the wood with stain, oil, or iron sulfate.
5. A light, iridescent driftwood is achieved by colorwashing the wood. Brush on diluted white water-based paint and then wipe most of the paint off again with a cloth.
6. Another option is to give the lightly sanded wood a brush of white color using an almost dry paintbrush and a light hand. This will lighten the wood and enhance any irregularities.

Furniturus mobilis

Large wheels with spokes instead of regular legs make furniture more exciting. Wheels from an old-fashioned baby carriage look perfect with this coffee table made from rough, old floor-boards. It's quick to make and looks amazing!

COFFEE TABLE

Get an old baby carriage online or at a thrift store and use the wheels to make mobile furniture. It's easier to adapt your carpentry according to the measurements of the wheel axle you already have; otherwise, you can probably get a new axle made from a local workshop.

MATERIAL

- Tabletop: planks, with or without tongue and groove, at least 1 inch (25 mm) thick and about 40–47 inches (100–120 cm) long, with a combined width of 25½ inches (65 cm).
- Horizontal crosspieces: 2 pieces woodboard at 1 x 6 x 23 ½ inches (28 x 120 x 600 mm)
- Standing crosspieces: 2 pieces of lumber at 2 x 8 x 17 inches (69 x 190 x 430 mm)
- Wooden braces: 2 pieces at 2 x 2 x 12 inches (45 x 45 x 300 mm)
- Wheels from an oldtime baby carriage—2 pairs on their existing axle—or as an alternative, the smallest size bicycle wheels you can get hold of
- Metal clamp: 4 clamps or U-shaped staple nails
- Wood screws, flathead
- Wood glue

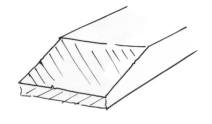

TOOLS

- Jigsaw
- Sander
- Mitre saw
- Power drill, drill and driver bits

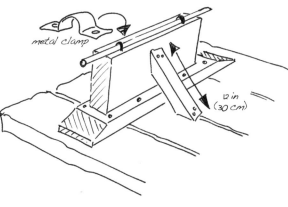

metal clamp

12 in (30 cm)

HOW TO

1. You can use almost any type of wooden board for the table top, preferably old and coarse recycled wood that has been worn a little, as long as you have enough to make a table top that is 25½ x 40–47 inches (65 x 100–120 cm) in size. You can make the boards look extra worn by using a bit of man-power. Hack, saw unevenly, chip with a knife, and then sand until the planks are smooth.

2. For a neater appearance, saw the ends of the horizontal crosspieces at an angle. The ends on the braces are cut at a 45 degree angle. Sand and shape the sharp edges on the crosspieces and braces.

3. Glue the standing crosspieces on the long side, centered on the horizontal crosspieces. When the glue has dried, you can make it more solid with a few screws from the back of the horizontal crosspieces.

4. Place the boards for the table top on a flat surface, back facing upward, and glue the horizontal crosspieces across the boards about 7–8 inches (17–20 cm) in from the short ends of the table top. Strengthen it with a few screws.

5. Make the table a bit more stable with a brace between the table top and standing crosspieces. Attach the wheel axle under the standing joist, using the metal clasps or the U-shaped staple nails.

6. Paint the frame. Old boards take on a nice, dark wood color if you simply treat them with a wood oil.

Military Madness

A few of my favorite bargains came from army surplus stores; these sell old military items at a great discount. You can find both old items and new, unused pieces very cheaply, and if there's one thing the army is good at, it's quality!

I'm sure you're curious to know what on earth I was looking for in an army surplus store! Well, over the years I've picked up a bunch of fantastic things: a pair of genuine rubber boots, some spacious duffel bags, and even a cool vintage bobber motorcycle helmet! For a while, I had my eye on a creamy white scooter displayed in the corner, but for the most part I stick with the cheaper things.

With some imagination, much of the army's discarded surplus can be used again. If you don't have one of these stores in your neighborhood, you can still capture the military look while using things purchased at other stores.

MANY SHADES OF GRAY

Don't hold back! Let your creativity go wild and sew a rough quilt from worn, old pieces of fabric. Mix and match with no real thought behind it; rip squares to get a rough edge and piece them together in an erratic fashion. Place large patches over dirty marks and holes. Bear in mind, however, that this quilt is made from old duffel bags that were probably lying around in old warehouses for years, so be sure to wash them before you start sewing.

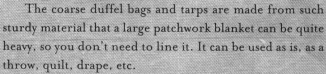

The coarse duffel bags and tarps are made from such sturdy material that a large patchwork blanket can be quite heavy, so you don't need to line it. It can be used as is, as a throw, quilt, drape, etc.

Rip the fabric to give the edge a nicely textured fringe, and place the pieces so they are slightly overlapping. Sew with a zigzag or straight seam with long stitches, or even a mix of both! Use an extra thick thread so the seams look decorative instead of sloppy. Mend any holes and cover stains with large patches; these should also be made from ripped fabric. Don't sew them too neatly. Let the seams be untidy, a bit too long along the edges, and go diagonally across the patch in the shape of a cross.

The duffel bags have large eyelets around the top edge, and you can use these as decoration. On my throw, I placed the edges with eyelets as a "hem" along the length of the throw. I decorated the throw with stamps and stencils to make words and random lettering.

A few things you might find in an army surplus store

- Duffel bags: durable and hardy material. The new ones are stiff and boring, but the frequently washed ones are beautifully worn and reminiscent of old tarpaulin.
- Military blankets, gray and beige: thick, coarse woolen blankets, incredibly warm and unused
- Linen towels: new, starched, creamy white linen, sometimes striped or checkered
- Disposable linens: long lengths of pretty weave.
- Sheets: top quality, high thread count, and reminiscent of fustian
- Buttons made from bone, or metal buttons with stars
- Glass test tubes with rubber plugs
- Leather straps
- Coarse sacks made of burlap
- Woolen socks
- Tin cans
- Buckets made from zinc
- Sturdy brooms
- Metal emblems—crowns, stars, crosses—that can be used as decor
- Camouflage cloths: a great present for the kids, perfect for building a fort in the woods

STENCILS AND STAMPS

The duffel bag's coarse fabric has a great, naturally faded look that works well with stenciled letters and numbers drawn in an old-fashioned style.

MATERIAL
- Textile paint, black and white
- Paper plate
- Masking tape
- Rubber foam + rubber band + wooden stick
- Stencils and stamps (can be found in craft stores)
- Metal stencils, can also be found in interior decorating stores and home improvement stores

HOW TO
1. Make your own tool for applying the stamps and stencil; fold some rubber foam around a wooden stick and secure it with a rubber band. Or, buy a foam brush from the art supply store. Pour some black and white paint on a paper plate. Place your fabric on a flat surface.
2. **Stencil:** Secure the stencil with some masking tape. Press the rubber foam into the black paint and blot on a piece of paper so that the foam's surface is not sticky. Blot/sponge over the stencil using a light touch. It's okay if the paint is slightly uneven and sparse here and there. If you think the result looks too densely black, lightly blot some white onto it.
3. **Stamp:** Use the rubber foam to dab the color onto the stamp. If you blot both a bit of black and white on the stamp's surface, you get unevenly colored letters that look slightly tougher.
4. Fix the color according to the instructions on the packaging.

If you want to make your own stencil of this crown, draw a template on thick, transparent plastic (e.g., a plastic file sheet) with a permanent marker. Use a sharp X-Acto knife and a glass pane or mirror underneath it to make it easier to cut out the stencil.

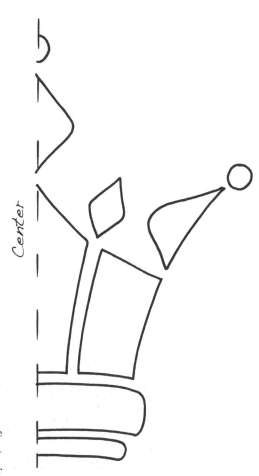

Center

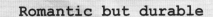

Romantic but durable

The thick, durable material from the duffel bags makes them perfect to use as upholstery for furniture.

For this armchair, I chose duffel bags of a more beige and linen color, and I combined this with crocheted doilies and linen fabric with a flower pattern.

If you're handy and enjoy working with your hands, you'll have no problems attaching a new cover to a chair or armchair that has smooth, fluid surfaces. The problems can be hidden under the surface.

1. Carefully remove the original cover so you can use it as a template to cut/sew the new cover. It's a good idea to take photographs during this process so you have a visual record of how the old cover was attached.

2. Remove the old and loose stuffing, then dust and vacuum thoroughly. This is where you might discover that you have more problems than just an ugly cover, especially if the interior of the chair is of bad quality. If it's a good piece of high-quality furniture, it might be worth the money to get it professionally upholstered. It might be hard to get the cost upfront for this, as the upholsterer won't know how much needs to be done until they start the work, but try to get them to give you an estimate if possible.

3. If you want to paint the wooden detailing, then do so now while your furniture is almost "naked."

4. The old cover can be taken apart and used as a pattern. If the new cover is being pieced together from smaller pieces of fabric, it's important that the seams are strong. Use extra thick thread and sew with 1 inch (2 cm) seam allowance. Preferably use double seams or one regular seam and then decorative, visible top-stitching for extra strength.

5. With the right accessories, the heavy duffel material can be given a more romantic look. I added a few patches with floral patterns to both cover a hole and make the chair more decorative. A few crocheted doilies made from heavy cotton wool can be stitched on using a basic straight seam or zigzag. A few numbers made with stamps or stencils take the edge off the romantic style and make the chair less cutesy.

6. Stuff the chair with new stuffing and take extra care around the sharp edges of the frame. Professional upholsterers use a more compact stuffing than the usual viscose rayon that you can get in the fabric store. Buy a few yards from a professional upholsterer.

7. Attach the new cover in the same way that the old one was attached, but use a staple gun with extra sturdy staples, ½ inch long, rather than tacks and upholstery nails—it's quicker and easier! Well worth the money for purchasing that staple gun. If you frequently do DIY projects, an electric staple gun is an even better investment.

8. When I removed the buttons on the back of my armchair I marked the placement clearly with a pen. The new buttons should be attached with a strong thread (preferably doubled). Use a long, thick needle with a sharp end. Pull the thread through the button and then pull both thread ends through the needle. Then push the needle through from the front of the armchair. In this way you get both the thread ends at the same time. Tie the thread around a bit of burlap to act as resistance.

9. Cover the back of the armchair with a "lid" of cardboard covered by the material. Heavy, sturdy cardboard, 1/12 inches (1–2 mm) thick, can be purchased from well-stocked office and art supply stores. Use the old ones as a templates to cut out the new ones.

SOFT FOR SITTING

Thick military blankets can be used for a lot of things but are particularly good as seat covers. The coarse wool is warm to sit on and can be used on wooden benches in cold weather. The wool is felted by a process known as "fulling," and you can cut and sew without having to zigzag the hems. If you want to make a neat edge, use a leather punch and crochet a single row of single crochets (see the description below).

CROCHETED EDGE

Use wool for needle size 4 to 6 and crochet hook 4/E to 6.

The wool is so thick that it's not possible to push a crochet hook through it, so prepare the fabric by punching small holes in it using a leather punch. Get one from a craft store; choose one that makes holes 2 mm in diameter. Punch the holes about ½ inch (1 cm) from the edge, spaced ¼– ⅓ inch (7–8 mm) apart. Make a round of single crochets (sc) around the edge of the blanket, through the premade holes. Then make a second round of sc.

Round 3: Loop = * 1 sc, 6 chain stitches (ch), skip 3 sc*—repeat around the whole blanket.

Round 4: * 1 sc in the sc on the previous round, 3 sc in the loop of ch, 1 picot = 3 ch, turn back and secure with a slip stitch (sl st) in the 1:st ch, 3 sc around the loop*—repeat to the end of the round. The "picot" makes a nice edge on each loop.

ROUGH CUSHIONS

The size of the duffel bags are perfect for making cushion covers. They're a bit too long, but you can just turn them inside out and make a seam across to get them to the right length. Letters and numbers painted with a stencil make cool decorations and give them less of a boring, militaristic appearance. The row of eyelets were used to make a nice fastening with the help of a thick string that was threaded up and down. I finished it all off with some big knots.

Cozy throw

Military blankets are the real deal! They're made from a thick, felted wool that is guaranteed to keep you warm. The blankets are designed for beds, which makes them big enough to cut in two to make cozy throws for the couch. If you want to add your unique signature to them, you can embroider, sew appliqué, or crochet a romantic border from woolen yarn around the edge.

TANGLED IN RAGS—A HOMEMADE CHANDELIER

Rags can be interwoven with a frame to create a cool lampshade. It can be made using any fabric, but new sheets from army surplus are starched and ironed and slightly more durable. This means the strips of fabric have a bit more crispness. You can achieve a great shape for your lamp if you hang the thinner strips at different lengths from the center of the lamp and attach a shiny glass prism to each end.

MATERIAL

- Welded wire mesh, with squares about 1 x 1 inch (2 x 2 cm) in size. You can get this at hardware stores. They are used as reinforcement when plastering and can be bought by the yard.
- Lamp ring, double, 10 inches (25 cm) in diameter
- Wire
- Sheets
- Glass prisms

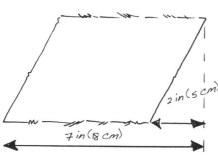

HOW TO

1. Cut the mesh, 10½–11 inches (27–28 cm) wide x 31½ inches (80 cm) long. Cut away any sharp metal bits so that the mesh has straight edges. Use the wire and "sew" the long edge of the mesh with large overcast stitches around the lamp ring. Then you can bend the mesh together into a tube. Place the short ends of the tube so they overlap slightly and attach with the wire.

2. Rip some long strips of fabric, about 2 inches (5 cm) wide. Wrap the strips around the mesh tube's top and bottom edges.

3. Rip 3–3½ inch (8–9 cm) wide strips. Cut the strips into short bits with angled and pointed short edges as per the template. Each strip should be threaded through the squares of the mesh. You don't need to tie the strips, as they are wide enough to keep in place in the tight space. As more strips are threaded through the mesh it will get so tight that all the strips are held together.

4. For the prisms, rip long strips 2 inches (5 cm) wide. At one end, fold the strip double and sew with a straight seam across the short end. Turn the seam inward so that it shapes the strips into a neat point. Press the seam and attach the prism to the pointed edge of the strips. The strips with prisms should be hung from the inner ring of the lampshade. Fold the strips around the frame and secure with a simple pin.

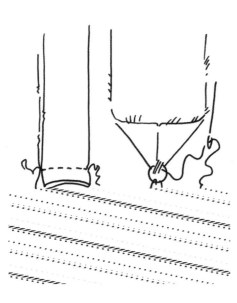

Shade: the lamp stand
"Ekarp" from IKEA has
an extra little shade
that prevents the
fabric from coming
into direct contact
with the light bulb.
If you use a different
lamp stand, choose a
low watt bulb and make
sure that the fabric
does not touch the
light bulb.

Neat with napkins

Thick linen towels from army surplus stores are real bargains and are great just the way they are. But they are also luxury fabric for bargain prices. A teatowel cut in two and hemmed makes a great napkin! They're also so durable that they'll last a lifetime . . . and probably your children's and grandchildren's, so why not make them extra special by adding some numbers sewn with cross stitch. I chose graffiti gray for the numbers and embroidered a silver-colored crown above each.

Cross stitch can be embroidered on any kind of fabric, using a waste canvas as a guide while stitching. Cut the waste canvas an inch or two larger then the actual motif. Position it on the fabric and baste along outer edges. Use a needle with a sharp point and sew with 2-3 threads of embroidery floss. When the embroidery is complete, moisten the waste canvas by spraying or sponging water on it. Then pull the canvas off, thread by thread.

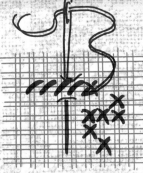

TIP

A super quick cheat for if your time and patience are running short: stencil the numbers on using textile paint instead.

TEST TUBES

Sort, organize, and store . . . for some strange reason, you can buy test tubes with rubber stoppers at army surplus stores. They are practical for storing small craft items, such as buttons, beads, and other small things. They're a lot more attractive than plastic tubs and are much trendier, totally in keeping with the love for all things science and nature that is around at the moment.

You can also use them as fun decorations. Pour some fine sand in each tube and add a strip with some inspirational words, a clever quote, or a secret message to pique a guest's interest and provoke some wonderful thoughts.

Romanctic and Elegant

Country romance style is perfect for all homes from cabin to castle. No matter the size of the house, the same light and airy base tone, worn and used furniture, tarnished silver, and unbleached linen look wonderful. Country manor style has a lot of typical shabby chic style—it's just a tad more elegant.

One hundred years ago there was a difference between country folk and the nobility. These days, you don't need to be a millionaire to decorate with golden mirrors and chandeliers. If you have an eye for a bargain, you can get the manor style at auction.

I say "style" as it doesn't have to be any special, fancy, or expensive antiques. Often you can get newly produced furniture in an old style for a reasonable price. Large, impressive furniture can also be gotten cheaply, as it needs more space than most people have and this equals a bargain for you. This is also the catch . . . if you want to get the old country manor feel, you kind of need large rooms and high ceilings!

If you don't have room for gigantic crystal chandeliers, you can still draw inspiration from the colors, texture, and surfaces to create a more subdued and country style that has a lot in common with shabby chic. If you already have a light country style at home, you can upgrade and get a hint of the manor house in mini format.

The worn and scuffed are part of the charm and we want to keep a relaxed environment, which is true to real life. The country manors of England are often owned by families who have inherited the family estate but lack the money to maintain it, meaning that that which once was fancy and luxurious is now worn by the sands of time.

GLITTERING GOLD

Silver and zinc, silver and zinc, silver and zinc . . . this has been the mantra for anyone who has loved country style over the years! However, gold is starting to make its mark; ideally its shine should be slightly dulled, more of a golden bronze or brass that hasn't been polished in a while. Large, ostentatiously embellished mirrors work well when wrought in white, gold, silver, gray, and black, as do crystal chandeliers and elaborate cast iron items.

SUBTLE & STYLISH ELEGANCE

Bright colors are visibly absent here as the country manor style is all about the more sober end of the color scale. It's classy, not cute! Dashing, stylish romance instead of pretty and whimsical! This elegant style works well in combination with rustic furniture and tarnished pieces.

· Neutral white, gray, and beige shades
· Accents of black and dark brown
· Dark red, gray-green, and gray-blue
· Wood and leather
· Details befitting a stately hall, such as busts and sculptures
· Old books
· Romantic black and white illustrations and photographs
· Pastoral motifs, toile de jouy wallpaper
· Silver, tin, and matte gold
· Beautiful, shiny glass and prisms
· Lace, coarse linen, quilted fabrics

ELEGANT & SPARKLING SHINE

Let it shine! Don't hold back with the mirrors, nickel silver, pewter, glass prisms, pressed glass, or anything that reflects light and shimmers and shines.

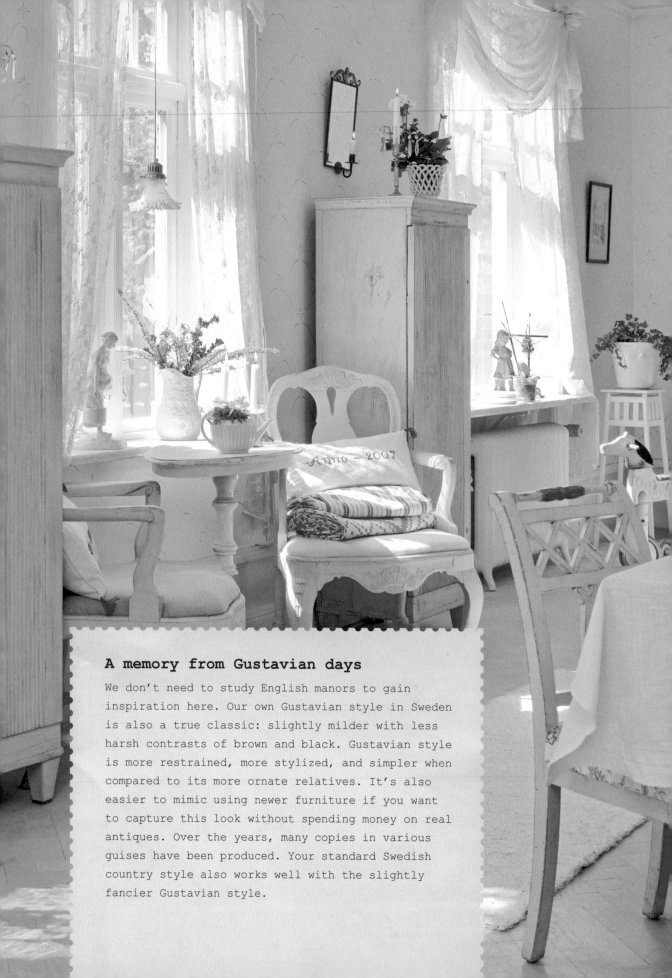

A memory from Gustavian days

We don't need to study English manors to gain
inspiration here. Our own Gustavian style in Sweden
is also a true classic: slightly milder with less
harsh contrasts of brown and black. Gustavian style
is more restrained, more stylized, and simpler when
compared to its more ornate relatives. It's also
easier to mimic using newer furniture if you want
to capture this look without spending money on real
antiques. Over the years, many copies in various
guises have been produced. Your standard Swedish
country style also works well with the slightly
fancier Gustavian style.

Play a bit of a trick

Real eighteenth century antiques
cost an arm and a leg but a similar
feel can be achieved with furniture
from a much later period if they are
painted the right shades and given a
nice border or beading. The
sideboard in this photo has typical
Gustavian raised décor on the doors
. . . or wait, maybe it's just an
illusion! Pernilla, the owner of
this lovely house, is handy with a
brush. The décor has been painted in
a slightly darker shade than the
rest of the sideboard. Very clever!

SALON FINERY IN SHABBY CHIC WHITE

Before you go at your furniture with paint and brushes, stop and think. Is this a valuable antique you're planning to attack? Right now, you may be all about white, but if you paint a great piece of veneered furniture, you can never return it to what it originally was. If it's a good quality, expensive piece of furniture, it might be better to sell it. You can use the money to buy some newer reproductions or furniture with damaged veneer. It's expensive and not really worth it to repair damaged veneer, which means you can paint and polish without a guilty conscience.

Reproductions from the mid-20th century that have been lined up in someone's "salon" can be made a lot more inviting with a dash of color and a worn surface courtesy of a bit of sandpaper.

GET INSPIRED BY GUSTAV . . .

- Gentle, neutral colors in white and gray
- Classically colored checkers and stripes
- Rag and warp rep rugs, even in the salon
- Monograms made from cross stitch and white embroidery
- Translucent lace curtains or classic roman blinds
- Candle sconces
- Porcelain blue, flame red, gray-blue
- Light and breezy flower patterns with elaborate vine motifs
- Silver, tin, glass, creamy white porcelain . . . you know, the classic country look

From châteaux to shacks
Stylish Silhouettes

Create a country manor look in your home with classical silhouettes. These give an air of the salon elegance of bygone days. Or create a more modern version with silhouettes of your own family.

Stylish silhouettes

The silhouette of a couple from the past gives your cushion a trendy look. Doll up your couch cushions, or why not keep tabs on which pillow belongs to whom? You can do this by earmarking the pillow-cases with a silhouette for the lord and lady of the manor!

TEMPTING TABLE DECOR

Lady, gentleman, lady, gentleman . . . why not label the napkins when setting the table? In the photo, the decorated napkins are linen, but you can use the same idea with thicker paper serviettes.

SUPER SALON CHAIRS

This is what you might call classy! These chairs came straight from the thrift store to my studio, where their legs were given some black paint. The old and stained cover was used as a template to make new, flowery covers in a pale color. I decorated the covers with empire-style silhouettes. These chairs will look great in any fancy salon.

When the wrong side is right

I find pale floral patterns to be really lovely. The flowers are like a faded memory, faintly reminiscent . . . almost like a whisper. Soft, pale fabrics are hard to find, but turn the fabric over and check out the back! On the test patch that has been nailed against the back of the chair, you can see what the fabric truly looks like on the inside of your new covers.

Silhouettes on fabric

With a computer

You need a scanner, an inkjet printer, a photo manipulation program, and transfer paper for light textiles, which can be bought in a craft store or stores selling printer accessories.

1. Use our silhouettes and scan them.
2. Adapt the size to the item you plan on decorating. You can do a test print on a regular piece of paper to check the size. If you do small images, you can easily fit several shapes onto the same A4 paper.
3. Print the silhouettes on the transfer paper and cut out with a small (2-3 mm) margin around the silhouette itself. Using an iron, attach it to the fabric according to the description on the packaging.

Without a computer

- In any copy and print store where they print images on T-shirts, you can also get images printed on your choice of fabric. The fabric should be pre-washed to ensure the print stays fixed in the washing machine. Bring your silhouettes and fabric to the store and explain what you want and they will help you.
- The silhouettes can be drawn onto a fabric with the help of the tracing paper, normally used for tracing patterns for dressmaking.
- If you draw your silhouettes on a light fabric, you can decorate and outline the silhouettes with textile paint and a brush or with special felt pens for fabric.

COLLECT YOUR OWN SILHOUETTE FAMILY

Black and white silhouettes are an effective and decorative way to portray your family. And it's easy to make them by yourself, as you only use one color: black!

MATERIAL
· Deep-edge artist's canvas (from craft stores or art supply stores)
· Black hobby or acrylic paint
· A thin artist's brush with extra long bristles
· A flat, straight brush

HOW TO

1. Prepare your motif. The easiest way is to tape a white paper that is the same size as your deep-edge canvas onto the wall of a dark room. Place the person whose profile you are painting on a chair some distance away and shine a strong light behind them. This should give you the silhouette as a sha-dow on the paper. Draw the contour with a pencil.

2. Make some fine adjustments to your sketch. You can simplify and enhance some features of the profile. Cut out the silhouette and place against the canvas. Trace the border with a pencil. Dilute the paint with a little bit of water to make it smooth and fluid. Use a thin artist's brush with long bristles to make it easier to paint an even line along the contour. A flat, straight brush is best for filling in any lar-ger areas. Allow to dry.

3. If need be, paint the black surface once more so it really covers the white canvas.

TIP
If you have some good computer equipment you can also photograph your subject in profile and then enlarge the image, crop it, and print it to the size you want your silhouette to be.

A pair of dames

This pair of ladies rejuvenated my old thrift store cupboard. The cupboard was black when I bought it, and I only removed the inset panels of the cupboard doors so they could easily be sanded down and painted in a gray and white checkered pattern. I finished it off by sanding it slightly to give it a worn effect and I used Mod Podge to attach printed paper silhouettes on as decor. When the Mod Podge had dried, I covered the surface in clear varnish and reassembled the doors.

Super storage

Regular cardboard boxes make the best type of storage when covered in paper, such as notebooks, pages from books, patterned wallpaper, or gift wrap. With a few musical bars on the boxes and a decorative silhouette, this storage solution went from plain to elegant in no time at all.

HOW TO

Use a regular glue stick, as it doesn't get messy and dries quickly. Apply liberally straight onto the box itself instead of the paper, one side at a time. Make sure you have covered the entire box before attaching the paper. Smooth out the paper and then glue on the silhouettes.

SILHOUETTES FOR MOD PODGE

The silhouettes can be printed as regular copies, but use drawing paper, which is more durable than regular printer paper. Photocopiers will make waterproof copies, but if you're using your own printer, make sure the prints are waterproof. Cut out the silhouettes with a small (2–3 mm) margin around the edge and attach using Mod Podge.

Glistening Gray

A slightly gray life? It's not as boring as it sounds—quite the opposite! Not only is gray a timeless classic, but it's even trendier today than it ever has been in the past. Don't hesitate to paint with gray. Using this technique, you can achieve shiny gray surfaces with a bit of a tarnished look in a heartbeat . . . as simple as that.

SHIMMERING BEAUTIES

Damaged by damp? Dirty? Worn? Just use your magic paint brush and abracadabra, your boring furniture is transformed into sober gray beauties. Okay, maybe it's not that easy, but almost . . .

GLISTENING GRAY

The more embellished and fancy, the more obvious the patinated effect of the white wax becomes. Old oak furniture looks especially good, as the short fibers in the wood become small, threadlike recesses on the surface where the white wax attaches. Any little holes, scratches, and marks will also be enhanced; this way it gains an exciting surface while at the same time looking aged.

HOW TO

1. Prepare the furniture that is to be painted. You can make it look extra worn by "damaging" it slightly. You usually don't need to do this if the furniture is old, but more recent furniture can be too smooth, making it visually uninteresting, even when it is painted. Hit at it with a bunch of keys or press it into a gravelly surface to add a bit of texture.

2. Larger holes can be mended and filled. Sand down the furniture with medium grit sand paper to make it matte. With oak, you can enhance the veined look by brushing the surface with steel wire. Dust and then wash down with TSP cleaner.

3. Tinted primer doesn't come ready off the shelf. You have to ask for it to be tinted. However, because the primer is an all-white ready-mix and not made to be tinted, there is a limit as to what shades you can get and it may not match the color sample that you find in the store exactly. My primer was tinted in the darkest shade of gray the store could achieve.

4. Paint as many coats of primer as you need to cover the surface and let the paint dry for a few days. Polish it with some fine sandpaper to smooth the surface.

5. Use a rag to add the white wax. Start by using a generous amount of wax to get it into all the nooks and crannies. A toothbrush can be useful for getting the wax into creases and any carved designs. Use a clean rag and wipe away most of the wax so that only a thin coat remains.

6. Let it dry and harden over night. Polish the surface, preferably with some wool, to give you a nice sheen. If you want, you can further protect exposed surfaces with a layer of clear wax.

- Sandpaper, fine/medium
- Prep paint cleaner, such as TSP or the more eco-friendly Citra Solv
- Filler, as required
- Stainblocking primer, tinted in a dark shade
- White wax for a tarnished effect (from craft stores; if you can't find it, look here: http://www.missmustardseedsmilkpaint.com/products/white-wax/)
- Clear furniture beeswax
- A good quality brush for varnishing
- Toothbrush
- Soft cotton rags
- Wool (an old sock will do)

RHOMBOIDS

Checkered patterns made from pointy diamonds are very current and are perfect to paint on large, plain surfaces such as table tops, doors, chair seats, and so forth. I finished off my own project by spattering small spots/speckles over the table top, which gives it an aged look and makes the surface come alive.

There are no hard and fast rules as to what measurements a diamond pattern should have. One of the parallel diagonals is longer than the other parallel but it's up to you if you want slightly chubby or long, pointy diamonds. Adapt the size according to the surface that you're painting. The table in the picture was slightly longer so I chose to make as many diamonds lengthwise as breadth wise, which meant the shape of my diamonds came naturally.

HOW TO

1. Paint the lighter shade first with as many coats as are needed to completely cover the surface. Allow to dry and cure completely.

2. Draw a rectangular checkered pattern with the help of a straight ruler and an L-shaped ruler. Draw diagonal lines through the squares to give you the diamond shapes. Use a pencil to draw faint lines; it's easy to get lost amongst all the pencil lines, so mark the diamonds you plan to paint.

3. Put masking tape on every other square that's being painted in a darker shade. Make sure you rub the edge of the tape to secure it. Put a dab of the lighter paint on a rag and daub the color along the outer edge of each taped square, as this blocks any cracks, stops the darker color seeping in under the tape, and gives your squares sharp edges.

4. Paint two coats of the darker shade and, while the second coat is still damp, remove the masking tape. Allow the paint to dry and cure completely before taping and painting the remaining squares.

5. Use an eraser to remove the pencil lines and polish the surface lightly with fine sandpaper to smooth it down.

6. Spatters/speckles: spoon up a small amount of paint on a paper plate and dilute it with a dash of mineral spirits/water to make it more fluid. Dip a toothbrush into the paint and do a quick test run by spattering a little paint onto a newspaper. You do this by pulling a finger through the brush. The brush's bristles spring back and shoot the paint on to the surface. When you feel that you have a grip on the technique, start working on your painted surface. Hold the paper plate underneath to protect against dripping paint. Spatter small spots of light color on the dark paint and vice versa. Let it dry.

7. To finish off, protect the surface with clear wax oil or beeswax—or white wax like was used previously.

The Pride of the Forest

— can be found in the sock drawer

Trophies made from moose and deer antlers are a great way to decorate. Most of us prefer to buy them second-hand rather than hunting the animals ourselves, or maybe we pick a more playful version from the interior decorating store? However, if you're handy, you can make them yourself

THE PRIDE OF THE SOCK FOREST

This proud moose is a real softy—made from a thick sock, which is easy to shape into the moose head and neck. This brown sock was found at the army surplus store, but you can find them just about anywhere; gray socks also work.

MATERIAL
- 1 pair of thick wool socks with an 8½–10 inch (22–25 cm) long foot for a small moose, 12 inches (30 cm) for a large one.
- Extra durable thread in a matching color
- Antlers: 8 x 27½ inches (20 x 70 cm) of velour or felt
- Buttons for the eyes, ½–¾ in (15–20 mm) in diameter
- Stuffing
- Wooden board, ¾ x 10 x 13 ¾ inches (18 x 250 x 350 mm) in size
- Masonite, 6 x 8 inches (15 x 20 cm)
- Craft paint or wood stain

TOOLS
- Needle + scissors
- Jigsaw + sandpaper
- Drill
- Paint brush + glue gun

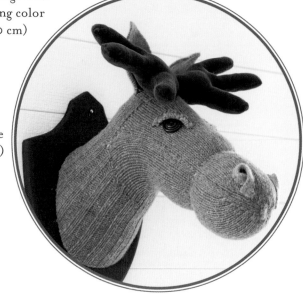

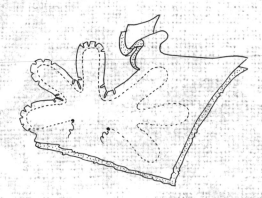

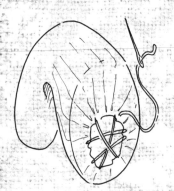

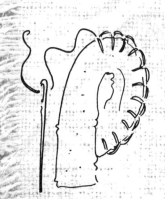

HOW TO (TEMPLATE AT THE END OF THE BOOK))

Wash and tumble dry one sock to felt it and cut all the small parts from this sock. Use the other—unwashed—sock for the moose's head.

1. Using a jigsaw, make the trophy's base from the wooden board. Drill holes so you can hang it up. Sand down all the surfaces and stain it in a shade of your choice with craft paint diluted with water or wood stain. Saw an oval-shaped piece from the masonite.

2. Stuff the sock with the filling to make it firm and easy to shape. The neck of the sock should be pulled over the oval masonite so that the sock is stretched and the neck is given a wide base. Place the board at an angle in the sock so that the head of the moose leans nicely. The more angled the board is placed inside the sock, the more the moose will appear to lift his head. Sew together the opening of the sock with large crisscross-stitches.

3. Shape the moose's nose: baste around the foot of the sock, pull, and secure the thread.

4. Fold the velour, right sides together, and draw the shape of the antlers according to the template. Baste the pieces together and sew along the pencil line with seam size 2. Sew a three-step zigzag outside the straight seam. Cut out the antlers, just by the zigzag seam, and make small clips in the hem so that the antlers can be turned inside out. Fill with the stuffing and hand sew the opening shut.

5. Baste around the center of the antlers, pull, and secure. Sew the antlers onto the moose head by hand. The ears are placed behind the antlers. Shape the ears by making a fold at the lower edge. Sew by hand to secure.

6. Nostrils: cut 2 strips, about ½ x 3–4 inches (1.5 x 8–10 cm). Bend them into a tight "P" shape and sew by hand using blanket stitch. Sew buttons on to make the eyes.

7. The eyelids are cut along the straight lower edge, across the sock's own knitted stitches, which mean you can pull the stitches up a bit so they fray and resemble eyelashes. Bend the eyelid around the buttons to lift them up and give the eyes a three-dimensional effect. Secure with blanket stitches.

8. Attach the moose to the trophy board using the glue gun.

BRANCH TROPHY

Why not find the next-best antlers on a walk in the woods? Look for dry, bare branches with as many V-shaped off-shoots as possible. If you have a pair of pruning shears, you can tidy the branch up on the spot, cutting the branch to size to give you an antler-shaped branch.

HOW TO

1. Make the trophy backing by jigsawing the template from a piece of wood ¾ in (18 mm) thick. Drill some holes so you can hang it up. Also, make a block that is 1 ½ inch (35 mm) thick and 2½ x 2½ inches (6 x 6 cm) in size. On two sides of the block, drill two holes, centered in the middle, ½ inch in diameter.

2. Sand down all the surfaces and edges on the trophy backing. The block is shaped and rounded off by sanding it as can be seen in the picture. Glue the block onto the trophy backing and stain with woodstain or craft paint diluted with some water.

3. The "branch antlers" are carved with a knife at the end to make them fit into the block. Secure with wood glue.

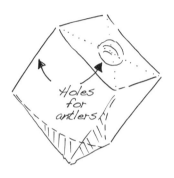

Holes for antlers

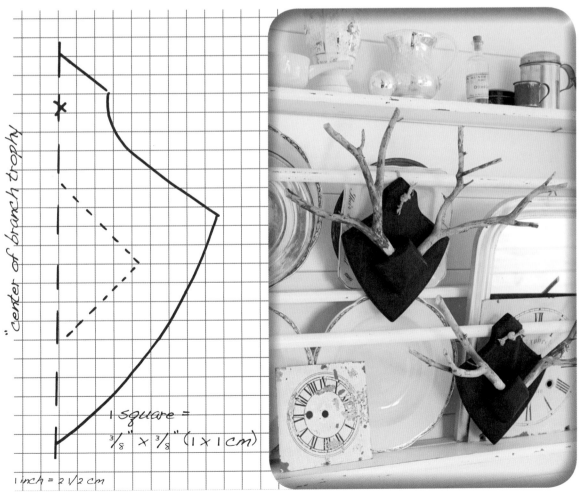

"center of branch trophy"

1 square = ⅜" x ⅜" (1 x 1 cm)

1 inch = 2 ½ cm

Creative Style Clash

Hard and soft, matte and shiny, old
and new, sweet and sassy . . .
try marrying the opposites!

Conceived in the 1950s, this rococo-inspired arm chair was originally used as seating in the salon, but time has passed and to fit into modern country style it needs some updating. Coarse burlap from the army surplus store gives this otherwise romantic white chair a new, rough uniform.

Furniture with a lot of carved embellishments can be hard to sand down. On flat but curvy surfaces, you can use steel wool or a brass brush if it's proving difficult to get into the nooks and crannies. Dust off and brush with some paint wash that doesn't need to be rinsed off.

The burlap may need to be reinforced with woven interfacing, pressed onto the wrong side of the material. Use the old covers as a template and cut the new pieces, sew a three-step zigzag to reinforce the edges of the cut-out pieces. Attach using a staple gun and hide the staples with some glued-on ribbon.

We've reached the end—I hope you've found the inspiration to indulge in some creative experiments and awesome transformations! Recycle, re-hash, and revitalize your home—and don't forget to have fun while doing so!

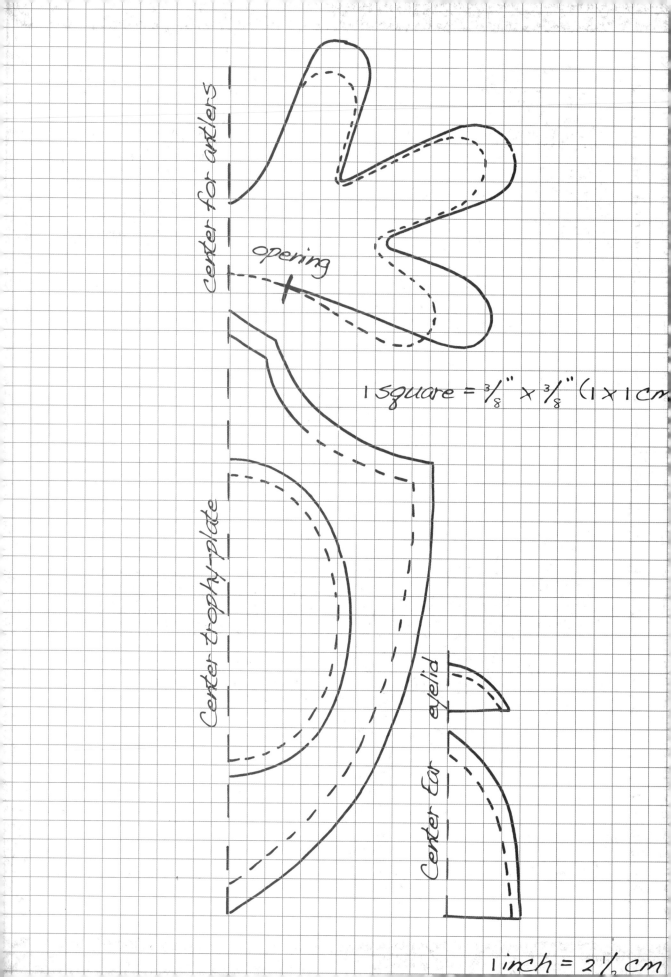

Center for antlers

opening

1 square = $\frac{3}{8}$" x $\frac{3}{8}$" (1 x 1 cm)

Center trophy-plate

Center Ear

eyelid

1 inch = 2½ cm